Penguin Masterstudies

Barchester Towers

Dr Graham Handley has taught and lectured for over thirty years. He was Principal Lecturer and Head of Department at the College of All Saints, Tottenham, and Research Officer in English, Birkbeck College, University of London. He is a part-time lecturer in literature with the University of London Department of Extramural Studies and also teaches part-time at Enfield Chace Upper School. He has examined at all levels from CSE to university honours degree and has published on Dickens, Mrs Gaskell and George Eliot. He has edited *The Mill on the Floss* and *Wuthering Heights* for Macmillan and *Daniel Deronda* for the Clarendon Press, Oxford. He has written studies of *To Kill a Mockingbird*, *The Pardoner's Tale* and *The Go-Between* for the Penguin Passnotes series and of *Vanity Fair* for the Penguin Masterstudies series.

Penguin Masterstudies
Advisory Editors:
Stephen Coote and Bryan Loughrey

Anthony Trollope

Barchester Towers

Graham Handley

Penguin Books

For Don, with warmest friendship and respect

Penguin Books Ltd, Harmondsworth, Middlesex, England
Viking Penguin Inc., 40 West 23rd Street, New York, New York 10010, U.S.A.
Penguin Books Australia Ltd, Ringwood, Victoria, Australia
Penguin Books Canada Limited, 2801 John Street, Markham, Ontario, Canada L3R 1B4
Penguin Books (N.Z.) Ltd, 182–190 Wairau Road, Auckland 10, New Zealand

First published 1987

Made and printed in Great Britain by
Richard Clay Ltd, Bungay, Suffolk
Filmset in 9 on 11 pt Monophoto Times

Contents

Acknowledgements

I am grateful to the many critics who have written, often with great enthusiasm and insight, on *Barchester Towers* in particular and on Trollope in general. Wherever possible, I have indicated any debt to them by quotation or reference.

On a personal level, I must thank Anne Dangerfield for a critical reading of this study and for helpful suggestions arising from it.

Note: All quotations are taken from the Penguin English Library Edition of *Barchester Towers* edited, with an introduction and notes, by Robin Gilmour, and a preface by J. K. Galbraith.

Introduction: Trollope's Life and Works

Anthony Trollope was born on 24 April 1815 in Keppel Street, Russell Square, London, the child of Thomas Anthony Trollope and his wife Frances, née Milton. His father was a practising barrister, and held the lease on a villa which he had designed and built on farmland at Harrow-on-the-Hill. Trollope and his brothers were sent initially to Harrow, their father's intention being that after a few years they would go on to Winchester, his old school. But Mr Trollope's irascible, argumentative nature soon cost him his practice and a potential inheritance, and the family settled in somewhat impoverished circumstances in Harrow Weald.

The father, something of a tyrant at home, devoted himself incompetently to farming and also to writing a 'universal dictionary of ecclesiastical terms'. His son Anthony, who was removed from Harrow when he was ten, went to a small private school and then to Winchester, where he joined his elder brother Tom. The latter acted as his tutor, mentor and tormentor, for 'as a part of his daily exercise, he thrashed me with a big stick', Trollope was to write years later. His childhood was miserable, his anguish compounded because he was big, 'awkward, and ugly' and had many unpaid bills.

Meanwhile his mother, intent on making her family solvent despite their half-mad father, took some of them to Cincinnati, Ohio. Here she hoped to set up what James Pope-Hennessy aptly says 'would now be called a boutique, to sell gewgaws, bric-à-brac and imitation jewellery to the benighted inhabitants of Cincinnati, who were already over-provided with such emporia'. This hopeful journey took place at the beginning of 1828, and Mrs Trollope soon found herself in debt. She was, however, a woman of great resource and stamina. She returned to England in 1831, and succeeded in making literary capital out of her failure. Her *Domestic Manners of the Americans* (1832) brought her overnight celebrity, set her off on a fecund literary career and, more importantly, provided her with the ready money to ease the economic burdens of her family.

In some ways this came too late to be of comfort or practical use to Anthony. He had been removed from Winchester in 1830 and returned to Harrow as a day-boy. According to one contemporary, he was regarded as 'an incorrigible dunce'. He was slovenly in appearance, his work was dirty, his manners were rude and his nature uncouth. At this time he lived alone with his father in the dingy farmhouse, although improvement, in the material sense, was to come with his mother's success. In 1832 they were able to move, and Mrs Trollope effectively became the family provider and wage-earner. Her husband was still in trouble, however, and fled the country to avoid arrest for debt. The family settled for a while in Bruges, where Anthony's brother Henry died in 1834. Although Mrs Trollope continued to write prolifically and to keep the family afloat through her earnings, that family was suffering grievous loss. Mr Trollope died in 1835, and his daughter Emily in February 1836. Anthony, meanwhile, through the influence of one of his mother's friends, had obtained a clerkship in the General Post Office. He made this, and literature, his career, and rendered distinguished service in his public role. He resigned from the Post Office in 1867, by which time he had achieved the eminence he coveted as a writer.

Initially Trollope struggled on a small salary and a deprived social life. His mother continued to produce the books of travels and manners by which she had made a quick reputation, but supplemented these with a regular flow of novels in the gothic, social, industrial and society modes. She moved first to Cumberland and then to Florence in 1844, where she died in 1863. Anthony's early years in the Post Office were characterized by a feeling of being useless and unwanted. His salary was ninety pounds a year, and he was often in debt to his landlady, sometimes being reduced to borrowing from a moneylender. As he records in *An Autobiography*, he was 'so little able to bear poverty' wanting, as most people do, to be liked, respected, popular. He found office life tedious, but with the setting up of a new group of surveyors' clerks whose activities were spread throughout Britain, Anthony seized his opportunity. He volunteered for a post in Ireland, much to the delight of his superior, Colonel Maberley, and started his work there in September 1841. His salary was increased, his expense allowance was generous, and the change signalled a turning point in his life. He travelled widely in Ireland and used his experiences there as the basis for his private career. He was able to take up hunting, a sport which gave him pleasure for most of the rest of his life and from which he was to incorporate scenes into his novels and stories. He looked back on his Irish days much later as being 'altogether a very jolly life'.

He began his first novel, *The Macdermots of Ballycloran*, in 1843 (published in 1847), met his future wife near Dublin (he married Rose Heseltine in 1844) and inspected the wide areas under his surveillance. He was not happy with his first novel, saying in the *Autobiography* that he felt certain that 'the book would fail, and it did faily most absolutely'. In financial terms this was true, but he was undeterred and continued to work on his second novel, *The Kellys and the O'Kellys*, which was issued in 1848. This shows a considerable advance in structure and in characterization. The reader's attention is cunningly divided between the fates of two disparate heroines, Fanny Wyndham and Anty (Anastasia) Lynch. The novel is notable, too, for its authentic scenes of Irish life and for the presentation of the evil, but credible, Barry Lynch, who tries to murder his sister Anty for fear that she will marry, and thereby prevent him from enjoying what he sees as his inheritance. The subtlety which is present in Trollope's later characterization is absent, but the narrative pace, full of incident and dramatic interactions, shows Trollope as already an assured writer in command of his materials.

Trollope was in Ireland throughout the great potato famine of 1845–7, conveying the terrible atmosphere of it much later in his novel about the period, *Castle Richmond* (1860). Meanwhile, his first son Henry was born in 1846 and a second, Frederic, in 1847. His mother visited him in 1849, and he found time to write an unsuccessful historical novel, *La Vendée*, which was published in 1850. He began, but did not complete, a guide book on Ireland, and wrote a play, *The Noble Jilt*, which was neither published nor acted. It is, however, of interest because Trollope later reworked the plot into the first of his 'Palliser' novels, *Can You Forgive Her?* (1864).

Discouraged by the poor reception of his writing, Trollope returned to England in his public capacity to reorganize postal services in the south west. Again the work, and in particular its location, was instrumental in providing Trollope with literary inspiration. He was an inveterate explorer of the counties that lay within his brief and, with memories of his early days at Winchester blending with current day-dream associations in Salisbury, Trollope began to create in his imagination the county of Barsetshire with its county town of Barchester. The sequence of novels which followed over the years is discussed in the next chapter, but the beginnings were slight. Compared with the vast novels, which were often issued in serial form, of the mid-nineteenth century (such as *Vanity Fair* and *Bleak House*) *The Warden* (1855) is modest in length, plot and treatment. It was, too, only a modest success, but it touched springs of interest and subjects of immediate contemporary concern – the widespread and influential role of the Church and the acrid tenor of the debate which had shaken it in the two decades prior to the publication of *The Warden*. The controversy attending the Oxford Movement, the defection of Cardinal John Henry Newman and Henry Edward Manning to Catholicism, the divisions between High and Low Church, these are the religious backgrounds which sometimes become foregrounds in Trollope's Barsetshire sequence. Without being partisan, he holds up the mirror to the Victorian Church, and it gives back the scenes and shadows of the times.

By the end of 1856 Trollope had earned just over £10 from *The Warden*. 700 copies were sold in five years, but after the impact of *Barchester Towers* and the success of the following novels, *The Warden* came to be valued in its own right. It is now seen not merely as a minor precursor, but as an artistic achievement which indicated the author's powers of characterization. Yet, initially, its relative failure led Trollope into another area. Deterred from writing a sequel to it, he wrote instead a strange but revealing book called *The New Zealander*. It was not published until N. John Hall edited the manuscript and issued it in 1971. He establishes its importance, and the present-day reader is left with a tantalizing 'might-have-been' had Longman's published it. Here Trollope becomes a critic of his own society, almost as if he had turned away from the fiction by which he meant to make reputation – and money. His title was derived from Lord Macaulay's prophecy of the 'New Zealander standing on the ruins of London Bridge'.

Professor Hall clearly shows that his manuscript is not the one rejected by Longman's reader as a pallid imitation of Carlyle, but a considerable reworking of it. There is a critical attack on the press, interesting in itself in view of Trollope's castigation of *The Times* (the *Jupiter*) in both *The Warden* and *Barchester Towers*. *The New Zealander* also carries criticism of the softness with which criminals are treated and the poverty of governesses, considers that England has become decadent, though Trollope defends those who mismanaged the Crimean War, and further pillories dishonesty in public life and the apathetic acceptance of it.

Trollope is opinionated, but forthright. It prepares us for the later bitter indictments of *The Way We Live Now*. I am not suggesting here that Trollope is a major social critic, but what is certain is that the uncritical view – still prevalent in so many appraisals and anecdotes of Trollope – suggesting he is cosy, socially limited, essentially the novelist of the middle ground who loves traditions and rejects change, is a blinkered one. The importance of *The New Zealander* is that it shows Trollope's social awareness. This is one of his major strengths, and he was able to channel it into his fiction. In *Barchester Towers* Trollope's social net ranges from the bishop's palace to Plumstead Episcopi and the deprivations of the Quiverful family or the impoverished sufferings of Mr Crawley at Hogglestock.

Barchester Towers signals the upsurge in Trollope's literary fortunes. It had taken more than eighteen months to complete, parts of it being written in railway carriages on his home-made portable rest. His next novel, *The Three Clerks* (1858), was based on his early experiences in the Post Office, while in the same year he wrote and published his third Barsetshire novel, *Dr Thorne*. An inveterate traveller, he always turned his travels to good account. He wrote *Tales of All Countries* and *The West Indies and the Spanish Main* in between two other novels, *The Bertrams* (1859) and *Castle Richmond* (1860). Trollope acknowledged his driving-force towards literary over-production, saying, 'I was moved by a decision to excel, if not in quality, at any rate in quantity.'

Having been sent first to Glasgow, then to the West Indies in the course of his duties, Trollope leased a house within twelve miles of London at Waltham Cross, Hertfordshire. There, during the next decade, he was to write the novels which substantiated his fame. When the *Cornhill Magazine* was launched in 1860 under the editorship of Thackeray, Trollope contributed the fourth of his Barsetshire novels, *Framley Parsonage* (1861), which had illustrations by the distinguished artist, John Everett Millais. Trollope was now happy in a settled home life at last, able to regularly indulge his passion for hunting, within easy reach of London and his job. He was beginning to emerge as a major novelist; more important, perhaps, he had become, in his own eyes, an English gentleman, far removed from those hobbledehoy days of his miserable youth. As James Pope-Hennessey says of his days at Waltham House: 'His salary from the Post Office increased, the contracts for his novels were better and better; he could now afford to live very comfortably and to entertain whenever he wished.'

Trollope became friendly with Thackeray and was elected a member of the Garrick Club in 1862. The same year saw the publication of *Orley Farm* (also illustrated by Millais). Of this novel Trollope was later to assert that those of his friends who 'are competent to form an opinion on the subject, say that it is the best I have written'. The plot deals with forgery involving a will, and the cases arising from it have been rightly criticized on grounds of legal inaccuracy. Despite this, *Orley Farm* is a great novel. Its characters, from the guilty and tortured Lady Mason to the English gentleman par excellence, Sir Peregrine Orme, are redolent of psychological truth. It is a study in noble love, misguided maternal love, and in generous and sympathetic love between the two women, Mrs Orme and Lady Mason.

It would serve little purpose here to comment on all of Trollope's writings from *Orley Farm* onwards. He was capricious as well as prolific, and one gets the impression that he was largely uncritical of his own work at the time of writing. About this time, too, he became friendly with George Eliot (she thought him 'the heartiest, most genuine, moral and generous of men') and was warm in his praise of her *Romola* (1863). Earlier, in 1860, he had formed a friendship with the striking American girl, Kate Field, which was to influence him for the rest of his life. It was a romantic affair. Kate was spirited, independent and, later, a committed lecturer on women's rights. She was also ambitious to write. A study of Trollope's letters to her shows not only the warmth of his feelings but the honesty which is one of his marked traits. He criticized a poem she sent him without reserve, and said of a prose offering, 'The end of your story should have been the beginning.' Perhaps because of his guilty feelings in the matter (though his wife Rose shared the friendship and corresponded with Kate herself), Trollope constantly urged Kate to marry. She resented this, and remained a spinster.

With the outbreak of the American Civil War Trollope obtained leave in August 1861 and wrote, inevitably, a book on *North America*. He was already contemplating another novel, provisionally entitled *The Two Pearls of Allington*. It later became *The Small House at Allington*, since the first title clashed with that of a book by Mrs Beecher Stowe, author of *Uncle Tom's Cabin*. This novel (1864) was the fifth in the Barsetshire sequence, Millais once more providing the illustrations. Shortly afterwards Trollope began another sequence of novels which developed as he became more deeply involved with his characters and situations. The first of these novels of political life was *Can You Forgive Her?* which Trollope regarded with great affection. The parallel plots concerning George Vavasor, his cousin Alice and Mr Grey on the one hand, and that of Burgo Fitzgerald, Lady Glencora and Plantagenet Palliser on the other, are consummately handled. In his *Autobiography* he was to observe that, 'Taking him altogether, I think that Plantagenet Palliser stands more firmly on the ground than any other personage I have created.' The question of moral choice or decision, as so often in Trollope, is strategically defined here. To concentrate on the Palliser plot, we find that Lady Glencora, who has married Plantagenet, becomes bored with his absorption in his political career and is on the point of eloping with her ardent admirer, Burgo Fitzgerald. The crucial moment occurs at a ball given by Lady Monk, Burgo's aunt. Palliser arrives just in time to frustrate his wife's intention and, although he has just been offered the post of Chancellor of the Exchequer, he declines it and takes Lady Glencora abroad. Their happiness begins.

The title of the novel was much criticized. It mattered little, for

Trollope was fairly launched on a new love; he had not yet, like Mr Slope, put off the old, but he proceeded to do so with *The Last Chronicle of Barset* (1867). His prodigious output continued through the mid and late 1860s, and he even published two books anonymously (these were *Nina Balatka* and *Linda Tressel*), almost as if he needed to assure himself that his known name was not needed for him to achieve literary success. The second novel in the political sequence was *Phineas Finn, the Irish Member* (1869), but the same year witnessed the publication of *He Knew He Was Right*. This is a compulsive study in psychological realism. Its theme is sexual jealousy, and in the power and incisiveness of its insight it rivals *Orley Farm*. Trollope exposes with a considered fatalism the jealous husband who eventually becomes mad. His own verdict on the novel was incongruously modest: 'I look upon the story as being nearly altogether bad.' It isn't. Michael Sadleir has noted the 'pathological study' which traces the tragedy of Louis Trevelyan and its disintegrating effect on his wife, a woman of independence and integrity. It is a dark novel, indicative of Trollope's variety and range, evidence of his ability to undertake a subject in depth which is both moving and sombre. Trollope's awareness of structure is evident too, and a balance is achieved through the happy love of Hugh Stanbury and Nora Rowley, Emily Trevelyan's younger sister.

Space precludes any full treatment of the Palliser novels, but they provide, through strongly individualized characterization and a graphic sense of moral and public situation, a close look at the political life of the period. Some of the characters are loosely based on the major figures of the time, such as Mr Gresham (Gladstone) in *Phineas Finn* and *Phineas Redux* (1874); Mr Daubeny (Disraeli), who appears in both these and in *The Prime Minister* (1876). There are convincing portrayals of obsessive characters, such as Mr Kennedy (*Phineas Finn*), or unscrupulous self-seekers, such as Ferdinand Lopez (*The Prime Minister*), but the triumphs lie in the range of positive women characters, from Laura Kennedy and Violet Effingham in *Phineas Finn*, to Marie Goesler who marries Phineas in *Phineas Redux* after having secured evidence which exonerates him from the murder of Mr Bonteen. Just as *The Small House at Allington* and *Framley Parsonage* are outside the cathedral close in the Barsetshire sequence, so *The Eustace Diamonds* is peripheral to the political series. But Lizzie and her machinations are compelling. Trollope referred to her affectionately as 'a cunning little woman of pseudo-fashion', and Disraeli is said to have praised Trollope for the 'happy lightness of touch in the portrait of your new adventuress'.

These are the main achievements of Trollope in fiction, yet one novel,

The Way We Live Now (1875), which is outside either sequence, is perhaps his greatest work. It is a bitter and unequivocal satire on his times, based on 'what I conceived to be the commercial profligacy of the age'. At the centre of the society web is the great financier Augustus Melmotte. Suitors flock around his only child Marie. Melmotte is a swindler on an international level, dealing, among other things, in railway shares in a fictitious company. Before his guilt is known he is selected, despite rumours, to stand for Parliament for the Conservative party. He wins the seat but, as his forgeries are exposed – he even tries to get his hands on his daughter's trust fund – he finds himself abandoned and ostracized by those who had courted him. In one of the finest scenes in the novel he insists on attending the House of Commons in a state of drunkenness. He is disgraced, and returns home to commit suicide. His figure bestrides a novel which has many memorable portraits. There is Lady Carbury, who writes and slaves for her blackguard son Sir Felix. Marie Melmotte falls in love with the latter only to be betrayed by his indolent selfishness. There is Winifred Hurtle, the American woman with a past who is in love with Paul Montague, himself in love with Hetta Carbury. The sub-plots subtly interact with Melmotte's spurious rise and decisive fall, and a comic sub-plot has the honest yokel John Crumb revenging himself on Sir Felix Carbury for making love to his sweetheart, Ruby Ruggles. For Trollope, society ruled by money is tainted: the novel is vibrant, telling and probing in its analysis of the various components which make up such a society – decadent aristocrats, dishonest editors, indolent men about town, financial manipulators, American opportunists – all these and their satellites are the degrading realities. Trollope is radical in this novel, though elsewhere that radicalism is turned on its head by his inherent conservatism. Despite the bitterness, Trollope's humanity runs through *The Way We Live Now*. Not the least of his achievements is his ability to make the reader *feel* for Melmotte despite everything, for his unscrupulousness at public and private level is balanced by a certain dignity in adversity and the poignant isolation which attends failure and the loss of face.

Trollope's prodigious output laid him open to attack by the critics, but, with an active social life, his political ambitions were stirred. He was persuaded to stand as a Liberal for the constituency of Beverley in 1868. Part of his election address read:

> The question which will next press upon Parliament will probably be that of the Education of the People. I am of opinion that every poor man should have brought within his reach the means of educating his children, and that these means should be provided by the state.

Like Thackeray before him, Trollope failed in his attempt to enter Parliament, though he always felt that to be a Member 'should be the highest object of ambition to every educated Englishman'.

By now he had resigned from the Post Office, and late in 1867 he accepted the editorship of *St Paul's Magazine*. Despite his electoral defeat, he continued to be fascinated by politics. In 1868 he visited the United States to help negotiate the Anglo-American Postal Treaty and also to promote International Copyright agreement between the United States and England. This was not successful. In 1870 he completed the translation of Caesar's *Commentaries*, decided to sell Waltham House and move to London; a year later he went to Australia for the marriage of his son Fred. He left behind the manuscripts of three completed novels and began a fourth, *Lady Anna*, the day after he set out. He also arranged to write a book about his experiences, which was published as *Australia and New Zealand* in 1873. He was to visit Australia again two years later, and one of the results of this second visit was a fine novel, *John Caldigate*, with its superb gold-mining scenes and at least one notable and unusual psychological study in Mrs Bolton.

In 1873 he moved to a house in Montague Square near Oxford Street. From now on he began to dictate his novels to his niece. He became increasingly deaf, and there were other indications of a premature old age. By the mid 1870s there was increasing criticism of his work, and *The Prime Minister* (1876) was the last novel for which he received a sum comparable to that of the great works of his middle period, such as *Orley Farm*. *The Prime Minister* endured some scathing reviews, but it is interesting to note that Tolstoy read it while he was writing *Anna Karenina*, and considered it 'a beautiful book'. Ill with a liver complaint, weighing over sixteen stone, Trollope began work on *An Autobiography*, which seems to have been written almost to himself, the instruction to his son being that it should not be published until after his death. James Pope-Hennessy has rightly called it a tantalizing book because it makes the reader 'more and more exasperated not by what he chooses to tell the world about himself, but by the enormous amount of personal feelings and intimate events which he has chosen to leave out'. For the Trollope student it is essential reading. Hennessy goes on to suggest that Trollope misrepresents himself 'as a dull, straightforward old party who wrote novels at a mechanical speed and with moralistic aims'. This view is too modest. The sense of honesty which is present in all Trollope's work graces the autobiography. The deprivation of his childhood is recounted poignantly but without over-indulging in self-pity. It is almost as if the old novelist is looking back in anger, but with a wisdom which has succeeded in eliminating bitterness.

As for the often-quoted practice of writing habits, his careful utilizing of time, his day-dream romances which were the prelude to his brand of fictional realism, his observance of the mechanics and disciplines of his craft, all these seem to me essentially expressions of the man's truthfulness to himself. There is a moral tone in his fiction, a consciousness of choice with its attendant self-respect or guilt. It is true that Trollope represents himself as a journeyman or a craftsman (the analogy with the shoemaker is often quoted); I suggest that, with becoming humility, he was both. *An Autobiography* is a riveting reflection of the man, and its tone is consonant with the tone of his best work in fiction – wise, warm, tolerant, sometimes sad or pathetic but always catching the experience of life in its sympathetic and emotional identifications. The only thing I find markedly missing is the humour, the fine comic sense which plays over a novel like *Barchester Towers*. It seems likely that Trollope's writing was a necessary release, so that his outward aggressiveness, frustrations, bluntness, biases and frequent irascibility were shaped into the considered prose which, at its greatest, is enlightened and urbane. He transmuted life into literature, and in doing so he created the illusion of life itself.

In 1877 Trollope went to South Africa, wrote about it, and felt very homesick, observing that 'The grandest scenery in the world to me would be Montague Square'. Astonishingly, in his last five years he wrote eight novels, with *The Landleaguers* left incomplete. Gradually his health began to fail. In 1878 he regretfully gave up hunting. He had become subject to asthmatic attacks and, in 1880, the Trollopes moved to Harting, near Petersfield, in West Sussex. He suffered from angina pectoris, a severe hernia, and also had a slight stroke. Despite these setbacks he continued to work himself hard, writing a monograph on Thackeray which reflects his reverence for that great writer.

The only book which shows any evidence of a decline is *The Fixed Period*, which was issued in *Blackwood's Magazine* from October 1881 to March 1882. The setting is an island in the Pacific, the basic theme being that of euthanasia for people over the age of sixty-seven (it is a strange but perhaps deliberate irony that Trollope himself was sixty-seven in 1882). This is the law of the fixed period. Fortunately, the islanders resume their British sovereignty, and the law is repealed. The work is totally uncharacteristic of Trollope's usual style, tone and effect, but at least it shows the fertility of his imagination in this late period of his writing career. One sentence remains pathetically – even bravely –

applicable to himself in this year of his own death: 'Men should arrange for their own departure so as to fall into no senile weakness, no slippered selfishness, no ugly whinings of undefined want, before they shall go hence and no more be thought of.'

With old age upon him, his fiction reflects his concern with it. *Mr Scarborough's Family* and *An Old Man's Love* (both published posthumously) underline his imaginative acceptance. The first comprises a telling psychological study of old Mr Scarborough himself. The second relates, with moving insight, the jilting of William Whittlestaff, his later life and love, and his renunciation of his ward in favour of her young lover.

Trollope visited Ireland in 1882 having begun work on *The Landleaguers*. He was often in pain, suffered from shortage of breath, and was obliged to return to London. There, at the beginning of November 1882, he suffered a stroke after dining out at his brother-in-law's house in Pimlico, but he lingered on for another five weeks. Posterity has accorded him many tributes, some of which are of dubious value. His name, and by analogy his novels, conjure up a cosy cult, with his prose preserving the upper-middle-class-cum-aristocratic image of 'the way they lived then'. During the Second World War he was read in railway carriages and air raid shelters, his fictional world providing a permanence for those who feared for their own. Politicians and clerics admire him; his best-known works have given him a wider currency by being adapted for television. The vast Trollope canon has provided a critical industry which, if not as large as that devoted to Henry James, Thomas Hardy, D. H. Lawrence or James Joyce, has at least gone some way towards establishing his right to be regarded as one of the great Victorians. In the following pages of this commentary I hope to underline that right in artistic and humanitarian terms, and to indicate the nature of a greatness which still has its doubters and often its detractors.

1. Barsetshire

Henry James wrote in his *Partial Portraits* (1888) that 'Trollope will remain one of the most trustworthy though not one of the most eloquent of the writers who have helped the heart of man to know itself'. The Barsetshire novels prove the first assertion and deny the second unequivocally. In those six novels Trollope is remarkably and consistently fluent, and he is consistent, too, in his treatment and revelation of the human heart. The inception of the sequence is given in *An Autobiography*:

> In the course of the job I visited Salisbury, and whilst wandering there one midsummer evening round the purlieus of the cathedral I conceived the story of *The Warden*, – from whence came that series of novels of which Barchester, with its bishops, deans, and archdeacons, was the central site ... I never lived in any cathedral city, – except London ... My archdeacon ... for whom I confess I have all a parent's fond affection, was, I think, the simple result of an effort of my moral consciousness ... But my first idea had no reference to clergymen in general. I had been struck by two opposite evils ... The first evil was the possession by the church of certain funds and emoluments which had been intended for charitable purposes, but which had been allowed to become incomes for idle church dignitaries ... The second evil was its very opposite ... I had also often been angered by the undeserved severity of the newspapers towards the recipients of such incomes, who could hardly be considered to be the chief sinners in the matter.
>
> (*An Autobiography* I, 123–5)

This full statement, dressed though it is with the advantages of hindsight, shows Trollope's moral concern and his essentially secular approach. *The Warden*, the first of the sequence, like each of the other novels, can be read in isolation for the sheer enjoyment of Trollope's narrative skills, his powers of characterization, his analysis of situation, his omniscient control, his humour, humanity and what I choose deliberately to call love. I use the word because it is emblematic of Trollope's relationship with his characters. This 'love' is one of the reasons why there is an enhanced, broader and deeper enjoyment of Trollope if the reader is saturated in the overall Barsetshire experience. In this chapter I am not too concerned with the group comprising *Dr Thorne*, *Framley Parsonage* or *The Small House at Allington*, since none of these is centrally involved with the bishop's palace, Hiram's Hospital, the Quiverfuls before the move from Puddingdale, the archdeacon out at Plumstead Episcopi, or the Crawley's suffering at Hogglestock – all ingredients of *The Warden*, *Barchester Towers* and *The Last Chronicle*. There is, of course, some interaction between each group. For example, Dr Thorne is a member of the commission which is to question Mr Crawley in *The Last Chronicle*, while Trollope himself wrote of *Framley Parsonage* that the story was 'thoroughly English. There was a little fox-hunting and a little tuft-hunting, some Christian virtue and some Christian cant. There was no heroism and no villainy. There was much Church, but more love-making. And it was downright honest love . . .' (*An Autobiography*, I, 191).

This statement is in fact definitive of the main group too. In *Framley Parsonage* Lucy Robarts eventually marries Lord Lufton. He had been intended by his mother for Griselda Grantly, the archdeacon's younger daughter, a beauty who soon married Lord Dumbello, a stupid man of status. *Framley Parsonage* is superbly constructed, the weakness of Mark Robarts and the pride, dignity and thoroughgoing unselfishness of Lucy being particularly worthy of note. *The Small House at Allington* is a largely romantic masterpiece. Lily Dale is a memorable heroine suffering in her true love for the worthless Aldolphus Crosbie. There are some vivid London office scenes involving Sir Raffle Buffle and Lily's young suitor, Johnny Eames. The latter is inadvertently, but nevertheless deeply, involved with his landlady's daughter, Amelia Roper, who had 'sometimes the plumage of a dove' though she could (and did) 'occasionally ruffle her feathers like an angry kite'. This major novel has its main focus of sympathy on Lily but, and this is Trollope's great strength, the minor characters are depicted as convincing individuals.

The Warden was assessed by Joseph Cauvin, reader for William Longman. His remarks on *The Precentor* (its original title) are worth noting here:

> . . . such is the skill of the author that he has contrived to weave out of his materials a very interesting and amusing tale . . . The characters are well drawn and happily distinguished; and the whole story is pervaded by a vein of quiet humour and (good-natured) satire . . . The description of *The Times* under the nom de guerre of *Mount Olympus*, (*sic*) I will back against anything of the kind that was ever written for geniality and truth. In one word, the work ought to have a large sale.
>
> (*Letters* I, 38–9)

It didn't, but the appreciation is positive, unlike the same reader's almost wilful misjudgement of *Barchester Towers*. The germ of *The Warden* is the misuse of a charitable trust. Trollope had followed the controversy in *The Times* over the medieval almshouses on the fringe of Winchester known as St Cross. These almshouses and their wardenship were held in the gift of Lord Guildford. The warden had a very good income from the trust, and this had grown over the centuries to positive wealth. The controversy raged over whether the inmates rather than just the warden should be entitled to the accumulated moneys. From this beginning Trollope posed the moral problem facing the warden in his novel with unerring insight and sympathy.

Trollope took an innocent, elderly, devoted warden, with an income of £800 a year, and twelve bedesmen within his care who were each paid one shilling and fourpence a day. This is the focal point of a press struggle for 'justice' (how strikingly modern it is in emphasis) as represented by the person of Tom Towers of the all-powerful newspaper the *Jupiter*. Opposing this is the warden's son-in-law, the bishop's son, Archdeacon Grantly. He is proud, well born, good-living, with a tinge of arrogance and more of irascibility. The situation is complicated by the fact that Mr Harding's (the warden's) younger daughter is being courted by a surgeon of independent views who subscribes to a keen, but not spurious, opportunist or journalistic sense of justice. A practical idealist, Johnny Bold believes that the affairs of the foundation administering the hospital have been mismanaged. However, Bold is a man of conscience and a man of powerful feelings, and he responds to Eleanor's pleas on her father's behalf by telling her that he loves her. He follows this by withdrawing his lawsuit against Mr Harding, and then is honourable enough to go to the archdeacon and inform him that he has retracted. It is part of Trollope's insistent irony that the archdeacon affects to misunderstand his motives, and treats him with an arrogant contempt which displays a wilful self-indulgence of triumph. He tells Bold that the attorney-general, Sir Abraham Haphazard, believes that Mr Harding 'is as safe in the hospital as I am here'. He further assures Bold that he will not be allowed to withdraw. Their dialogue, with its attendant temper and temperature, shows Trollope at his very best:

> 'I have nothing further to say or to hear,' said the archdeacon. 'I'll do myself the honour to order your horse' and he rang the bell.
>
> 'I came here, Dr Grantly, with the warmest, kindest feelings –'
>
> 'Oh, of course you did; nobody doubts it.'
>
> 'With the kindest feelings – and they have been grossly outraged by your treatment.'
>
> 'Of course they have – I have not chosen to see my father-in-law ruined; what an outrage that has been to your feelings!'

'The time will come, Dr Grantly, when you will understand why I called upon you today.'

(Chapter 12)

This is good, crisp dialogue, the character of each man compressed within the situation. The archdeacon is so often bloody-minded and wrong-headed. John Bold, also proud, is exercising admirable restraint, but the masterly effect of this exchange is that neither man understands, or tries to understand, the truth which has brought about the situation. Each stance is obdurate, and the result is fixity of purpose and absence of communication that admits of no rational influence. The archdeacon is intent on humiliation and revenge; John Bold is intent on self-consciously doing the right thing and to be seen to be doing the right thing. These subtleties lie behind the words.

Trollope excels at dialogue which brings the reader into intimate identification with character, and this extract anticipates the fuller revelations which underlie so many of the exchanges in *Barchester Towers*. Of outstanding significance in the latter is Madeline's finely contrived and blunt explanation to Eleanor of the state of her (Eleanor's) heart and that of Mr Arabin's. We might also consider any of the conversations between Bishop and Mrs Proudie, between Mrs Proudie and Mrs Quiverful, or an early conversation between Mr Slope and Eleanor. Cleverest of all in terms of pace and effect is the dialogue between Bertie Stanhope and Eleanor in which Bertie reveals that he has been put up to propose to Eleanor by his sister Charlotte, that dedicated family manager who wishes to see Bertie prosperously settled in life. Eleanor does her utmost to feel complete detestation when she hears Bertie's admission, but she cannot do so for Bertie, who is confiding in her because he does not want the responsibilities of marriage, is engaging and, in a way, behaving decently by telling her of the plan.

The Warden is comparatively slight, but this does not necessarily mean uniformly light. The novel shows one or two faults which will be dealt with briefly, but its tone is mature, urbane, compassionate and wise. The presence of the author's voice, whether in confidence, or employing narrative guidance or romantic rhetoric, is very much in evidence. It lays the ground evenly for *Barchester Towers*. The latter has perhaps more profundity of observation, a wider range of characters, a more developed sense of social and individual comedy. Mr Harding ages, and does so gracefully; the archdeacon waxes even more angry at the prospect of Eleanor marrying Mr Slope, but recants with relief and abundant generosity when he finds that she is going to marry Mr Arabin.

The signora conquers everyone except Mrs Proudie and Lady De Courcy, makes a fool of Slope and enjoys a number of scenes in which she is able to indulge her satirical verve to the full.

Trollope uses appropriate military imagery in the renewed battle for Hiram's Hospital. This imagery also symbolizes the clash between high and low church, the Proudie/Slope faction and the opposition led by the archdeacon. It is focused in the battle for influence over the bishop between Mrs Proudie and Slope, and in the battle for the deanery between the *Jupiter*-supported low church nominee Mr Slope and the high church nominees, first Mr Harding and then Mr Arabin.

The advance in structure of *Barchester Towers* is evident in the complexity of plot and an awareness of interactions which are handled with confidence and delight. Consider, for example, the archdeacon's reaction after the first meeting at the bishop's palace with Mrs Proudie and Slope (the bishop seems hardly to count) when 'Good Heavens!' becomes more of an expletive than a reflex exclamation. Consider the two chapters which constitute Mrs Proudie's reception and the bubbling comedy of Bertie's appearance and actions ('Bishop of Barchester, I presume?'). There is the damping of Mrs Proudie's pride ('at present it behoved her to collect the scattered *debris* of her dress') and her acidulous observations on Slope's fall from grace ('I am surprised you should leave my company and attend on such a painted Jezebel as that'). The sexual jealousy present in this is finely sustained in the ensuing battle between the prelatess and her sometime protégé. *Barchester Towers* displays the consummation of Trollope's powers in his handling of scenes in both private and public spheres of life.

Amongst the more aberrant qualities of *The Warden* are Trollope's satirical attacks on Dickens and Carlyle. Mr Popular Sentiment and Dr Pessimist Anticant (Trollope's caricatures of the former and latter respectively) would certainly respond to the Hiram's Hospital case, just as their counterparts in real life would have made – as Trollope does – fictional capital out of it. (Dickens at the time was taken up with the national mismanagement of the Crimean War, witness *Little Dorrit* (1855–7), where the Circumlocution Office is reared on nepotism and the applied maxim of How Not To Do It.) There is little doubt that Trollope, aged nearly forty and eager for literary success, was somewhat jealous of Dickens's virtual monopoly as the great popular communicator. The attack on Carlyle takes the form of a parody of his style and a specific focus on Carlyle's familiar areas of attack, such as indolent aristocrats, their appropriation of rents and the killing of game. Carlyle's rhetorical flourishes are stigmatized in a series of 'Ohs': 'Oh, my poor brother . . .

Oh, my political economist . . . oh, my loud-speaking friend . . . Oh, the serenity of Downing Street!' (Chapter 15). Mr Popular Sentiment's new novel is called *The Almshouse*, a composite reference to *Oliver Twist* (1837) and *Bleak House* (1852–3). Trollope's tone smacks of bitterness; his judgement is more than a little distorted, and he even refers sarcastically to the Dickensian mode of publication:

> In former times great objects were attained by great work . . . We get on now with a lighter step, and quicker: ridicule is found to be more convincing than argument, imaginary agonies touch more than true sorrows, and monthly novels convince, when learned quartos fail to do so. If the world is to be set right, the work will be done by shilling numbers.
>
> (Chapter 15)

Even more influential in the area of print is Tom Towers, the editor of the *Jupiter* (representing *The Times*). Trollope is castigating the press for its opportunist practices, its blowing up of issues, the terrible impact of publicity which can wound in a personal way. Thus Mr Harding is scarred because of his sensitivity, and we are somewhat relieved to find that in *Barchester Towers* Mr Slope cannot be made dean despite the fact that he has enlisted the powerful aid of the *Jupiter*. Obviously Trollope feels that the powers of Oxford, although they constitute a kind of clerical nepotism, are preferable to the propagandist insinuations of the press which are so widely disseminated as truth. His love of tradition is evident, and by the time he comes to write *Barchester Towers* he has gained in self-assurance, so much so that there is no need to snipe at fellow-writers. He has got the press into perspective. Oxford proposes and disposes. Mr Harding declines the Deanery, but a happy insurance lies conveniently to hand with Arabin. His nearby living at St Ewold's and his love for Eleanor have made him not merely Oxford's choice, but the reader's as well. Trollope manifestly delights in his own cunning sleight of hand. There are no loose ends in *Barchester Towers*.

Before we leave *The Warden*, however, we might look a little more closely at the classical analogies which Trollope employs. As always in Trollope they are an insistent mode of irony and commentary. Sometimes they are casual, even commonplace, as in 'the Elysium of Mr Harding's dwelling' (Chapter 1); sometimes they are of weighted significance, as in Chapter 11, which is called 'Iphigenia'. This chapter deals firstly with Eleanor's thoughts and sympathies on her father's account. The author asks: 'Was not so good an Agamemnon worthy of an Iphigenia?'. Eleanor sees John Bold and upbraids him for her father's suffering. She implores him 'to spare my father, to spare either his life or his reason, for one or the other will pay the forfeit if this goes on'. It is an impassioned appeal, and indicates the quality of Trollope's realism. Eleanor holds John Bold 'with her hair dishevelled, and her eyes all bloodshot' but he 'had never seen her half so lovely; he was amazed at the intensity of her beauty'.

Eleanor does sacrifice herself for her father, though anyone less like Agamemnon than Septimus Harding would be hard to imagine. That, I think, is certainly part of Trollope's irony, for Eleanor's sacrifice is her gain, her father's gain and, of course, John Bold's gain. Trollope closes the chapter with a succinct reference to the Aeschylean tragedy ('And so the altar on the shore of the modern Aulis reeked with no sacrifice'). The promise of future domestic harmony is a long way from tragedy, but by employing the analogy Trollope is establishing the perspective of his own material. Human appeal and sacrifice mitigate human suffering. There is a curious derivation from Thackeray here. In Chapter 11, the Iphigenia chapter, Trollope writes 'not so had Jephthah's daughter saved her father' before he proceeds to develop the Iphigenia analogy. Thackeray in *Vanity Fair* (a novel greatly admired by Trollope) has an Iphigenia clock sequence which refers to the pattern of sacrifices in that novel. Strangely Thackeray originally wrote 'Jephthah' (who had to sacrifice his child – see Judges 11) but deleted it and wrote 'Iphigenia' instead.

The tone of *The Warden* is a compound of kindliness, warm appraisal of character, and comic, satirical and ironic effects. As in *Barchester Towers*, there is a range of reference from the political to the religious. One quality each novel in the sequence shares is the Trollopian inventiveness, shown particularly in his choice of names both for people and places. From Quiverful, Puddingdale, Hogglestock to Sir Abraham Haphazard and Sir Omicron Pie, they have a Dickensian fecundity of imagination. The analogy is deliberate, for just as Dickens establishes an intimacy with his readers which is built on the positive virtues of unforgettable caricature – Mr Pickwick, the Artful Dodger, Mrs Nickleby, Mr Micawber, Silas Wegg – so Trollope does too, but with a somewhat different effect. In Barsetshire Trollope creates a world, and peoples it with families which have a vibrant consistency. When we first meet Mr Harding and the bedesmen, whose characters range from the erect pride of Bunce to the 'sour, ill-omened visage' of the subversive Abel Handy, we are aware of a family atmosphere, with quarrels, carping, loyalty, humility and arrogance. In a sense Harding is a father to these old men, who are his good, or recalcitrant, children.

I have chosen the word 'family' deliberately for I believe that it conveys the intimacy of association which Trollope achieves in the Barsetshire series. The sequence itself is the development of the families, and it is one of the reasons for reader involvement and identification. It begins in *The Warden* where the sense of family is most marked and where there is an admirable simplicity and directness about the writing. This is present in the retrospect of Chapter 1 and in the description of Chapter 16 which records Mr Harding's day in London. The friendliness, the sense of family is present, too, in the authorial voice, which is warmly confiding, perhaps another legacy from Thackeray which finds Trollope saying at the end: 'Our tale is now done, and it only remains to us to collect the scattered threads of our little story.'

From *Barchester Towers* to *The Last Chronicle* is a giant stride in terms of psychological effects and tone. To Trollope's own verdict on this novel – 'I regard this as the best novel I have written' – must be added a reservation regarding the inferior quality of the sub-plot, which involves the Dobbs Broughtons and Mrs Van Siever. Trollope acknowledged a partial failure in 'constructing with complete success the intricacies of a plot that required to be unravelled'. Nevertheless the novel has great strengths, seen in the character of Mr Crawley and his near madness in terrible poverty and unjust adversity. There is the deliberate contrast between his way of life and that of the archdeacon's, the latter's objection to his son's love for Grace Crawley (until he meets her and is completely won over by her beauty and modesty) and, superbly, the fall of Mrs Proudie and the abject pathos and isolation of her death.

Trollope has left an account of his decision to kill off Mrs Proudie after he had overheard a conversation between two clergymen maligning her in his club. Some critics have seen her death as a structural weakness, but it seems to me that what is important here is the account of the disintegration of the Proudie marriage. For the first time the bishop – pathetic, craven, the little committee man with the powerful and pushing wife – comes alive in his rejection of the helpmeet who has made him all that he wished not to be. Consider too, in this situation, the roles of the two outsiders, Mr Crawley and Dr Tempest, whose reactions give the bishop the index to his own deepest feelings. Dr Proudie is seen worn out by life and reduced by the arrogance of his wife, yet such is Trollope's compassion that we are made to feel for her in the anguish of her recognition of what she has done. In a novel which is largely about love – and Stephen Gill in his introduction to *The Last Chronicle* (Penguin) has correctly stressed the wonderfully simple expression of it which Mrs Crawley shows her stricken husband – the absence of love after a lifetime of exacting cohabitation leads to the bishop shutting himself away from his wife. There is nothing left for her to do but die, and Trollope's focus on the aftermath shows that the bishop is in some ways glad that it has happened. It is this kind of realism, and not the saccharine softness so often erroneously associated with him, which makes Trollope a great novelist.

Stephen Gill has also noted Trollope's 'cumulative power', and certainly the delineation of character, the developments and changes both in its interior aspect and outward relations is one of Trollope's great strengths. J. Hillis Miller has referred, in another apposite phrase, to Trollope's 'equable sympathy'. Trollope's own emphasis is clearly expressed in *An Autobiography*.

> A novel should give a picture of common life enlivened by humour and sweetened by pathos. To make that picture worthy of attention, the canvas should be crowded with real portraits, not of individuals known to the world or to the author, but of created personages impregnated with traits of character which are known.
>
> (*An Autobiography* I, 169)

These quotations are central to an understanding and appreciation of Trollope's art, and they surely indicate why *The Last Chronicle* is the jewel in the Barsetshire crown. If the 'cumulative power' of Trollope is seen in his searching exposure of the Proudie marriage, then it is also evident in the realism underpinning the pathos of the Crawley marriage. The 'equable sympathy' ensures that no character passes beyond the bounds of compassion. *The Last Chronicle* is a little short on typical Trollope humour, except in the sub-plot, but 'sweetened by pathos' aptly defines the relationship between Johnny Eames and the suffering – but how bravely suffering – Lily Dale. Henry Grantly and Grace Crawley do come together eventually but, as with Lily Dale, even here the realism outdoes the romance. Lily is a full and convincing character, obstinate, self-willed, warm, a prey to temptation but also to resistance, a woman divided against herself, rejecting love, apart from the one lost love which continues to dominate her emotions and to condition her reactions. Her confession to her mother that she still loves Adolphus Crosbie is one of the most moving moments in a novel which has a number of poignant scenes. Not least of these is that in which the archdeacon surrenders to the simple dignity and natural good-breeding of Grace Crawley.

The Last Chronicle encompasses a wide range of characterization, coupled with a psychological intensity which is unsparing in its dedication to truth. For the most part that truth is a sombre one. Here is the bishop after Mrs Proudie's death:

He was free now. Even in his misery, – for he was very miserable, – he could not refrain from telling himself that. No one now could press uncalled-for into his study, contradict him in the presence of those before whom he was bound to be authoritative, and rob him of his dignity. There was no one else of whom he was afraid. She had at least kept him out of the hands of other tyrants.

(Chapter 67)

This is not only a natural reaction to his wife's death, it also encompasses the duality of feeling in all of us, the knowledge of ourselves as we are and the sense of the image which we present to the world, a consciousness of what we are seen to be. This shows a deep psychological insight into the man, not so much the man who has escaped from crisis into being the kind of man he has wished to be, but a sense of immediate freedom from constraint, free (his word) from the pressures of marriage which made it impossible for him to be anything but a cipher. For behind this reaction there are implicit questions. Would he have become a bishop without her? Would he have survived being a bishop without her? Will he, in his freedom, withdraw from the responsibilities of being a bishop now that *she* can no longer sustain them? Trollope's emphasis is salutary; we do not know the answers, but such is our identification with character and situation that we want to know. This illusion of reality is the triumph of fictional art. The Victorian novelists often do not receive full recognition for their examinations of the consciousness. Trollope, like his great contemporary George Eliot, shows here that he is *inside* his creature. The bishop takes on a greater reality than he does in the verbal surrenders to and retreats from his wife.

I have tried here to trace associations within the main Barchester sequence in order to indicate analogy and difference, but there is one connection which exists as an imaginative and sympathetic adhesive. It is the essential spirit of Trollope's writing. Stephen Gill quotes J. Hillis Miller definitively here. Miller says of Trollope at his best that the novelist 'becomes invisible in a union of reader and narrator'. This is Trollope's fullest, deepest achievement; for the reader it constitutes an identification 'with the narrator's consciousness'. This intimacy embraces the reader's responses, conditions his reactions, and I suggest that this is high narrative art which has a moral basis. This omniscience establishes its own conventions of communication. It is not a sitting in judgement so much as an assertion that the judgement lies within, as in Adolphus Crosbie, for example, who comes to know himself and what he is really like after his marriage. It is a similar recognition to that of Bishop Proudie. Even when Trollope is idealizing – as with Lucy Robarts or Lily Dale or

Grace Crawley – we are made aware of so much that works. Divisions, difficulties, are made by the accident or tyranny of birth, of wealth or poverty, status or obscurity, and each or all are capable of being transcended by generous, sympathetic feelings which are sometimes elevated into enduring love.

2. Background: Historical, Church and Religion

There would be little point in combing through *Barchester Towers* to establish an exact chronology, though the action would appear to occur in the years 1852–3. P. D. Edwards has demonstrated by reference to contemporary history (in *Anthony Trollope: His Art and Scope*, pp. 224–5) the factual time corresponding to the Barset sequence, but there are inconsistencies here in the Trollope chronology, perhaps deliberate. Nevertheless the number of contemporary historical references in *Barchester Towers* gives an authentic sense of period and they are important in any full consideration of the impact of the novel.

Historical

On the first page of the novel there is a reference to an outgoing ministry: in 'the latter days of July 185–'. The government of Lord Derby actually fell in December 1852 and this brief Conservative ministry is obviously the one referred to. The Whig government of Lord Palmerston took office in February 1855 after the downfall of the Aberdeen coalition. Trollope is here combining, for the sake of fictional expediency, two major events known to his readers. The same chapter refers to the Ecclesiastical Commission which had been set up in 1835 and which dealt, among other things, with the stipends paid to bishops. Events of a broader nature are mentioned, in that the 'first threatenings of a huge war hung heavily over the nation' (p. 11). This must refer to the imminence of the Crimean War, which began in March 1854. Anglican anti-establishment personalities are mentioned, such as Whately and Hampden, along with their opposite numbers – 'brethren of Exeter and Oxford' (p. 18) – namely, the notorious Henry Phillpotts and 'Soapy Sam' Wilberforce, leading High Church Anglican administrators. Trollope has a neat remark on the possibility of ultimate rebellion by the bishop against Mrs Proudie in the analogy with the Neapolitans revolting against their king in 1848, one of the many rebellions in that year.

In a note on the 'University Improvement Committee' mentioned on p. 31 of the Penguin edition of *Barchester Towers*, Robin Gilmour points to an ambiguity, since this could refer to the Royal Commission of 1850 – which would be outside the internal chronology of *Barchester Towers* –

or perhaps the executive body of 1854 which was formed to set in motion the University Reform Act. David Skilton in his Introduction to *Barchester Towers* (Pan) has pointed out that the remark about the Begum of Oudh (p. 79) may refer to her visit to England in 1856. The debate between Eleanor, Charlotte and Bertie in Chapter 19 of the first volume contains a contemporary reference of considerable interest. This occurs on p. 160, where Charlotte asks Eleanor whether she is 'a Whewellite or a Brewsterite, or a t'othermanite'. John W. Clark observes of this and the ensuing conversation that it shows 'Eleanor's modest reluctance to discuss objects above her, then her orthodox but thoughtful piety, then Bertie's constitutional levity, and finally Charlotte's misanthropy' (*The Language and Style of Anthony Trollope*, p. 162). This astute comment underlines Trollope's capacity to make a contemporary reference a comment on character. Whewell believed that intelligent life did not exist elsewhere in the universe, and Brewster had questioned this. Their debate belongs to 1853–4, and Robin Gilmour points out in detail the irony of their respective positions.

The introduction of Mr Thorne into the narrative initiates a number of references indicative of his entrenched conservatism. There is mention of the fifty-three members who voted against free trade in 1852, and of the repeal of the Corn Laws some six years earlier, which led to cheaper bread and the expansion of trade, and is referred to on p. 192 as 'Sir Robert Peel's apostasy'. The position of Miss Thorne is equally fixed, for she is appalled by Catholic Emancipation (1829) and admires Lord Eldon, who was against it and against parliamentary reform. There is a finely ironic reference to Macaulay's 'dating a letter from Windsor Castle' (p. 304). This was written to his constituents in 1839, but Slope has the tact to omit the grandeur of the 'palace' from his letter to Tom Towers, thus forestalling any criticism of himself from that renowned fighter for democratic causes. There is even a reference to the Great Exhibition of 1851 ('a new pony chair that had gained a prize in the Exhibition', p. 496), and on the following page a note on the trial of a High Churchman in July 1856. There is little doubt that the range of contemporary reference, often with a slightly satirical tone reminiscent of *The Warden*, contributed to the success of *Barchester Towers*.

Church and Religion

Kathleen Tillotson is right when she says of the religious factions: 'It is of course the *ethos* of the parties, and particularly the concomitant social differences (slightly exaggerated) that Trollope emphasizes, rather than doctrinal differences; he hardly goes further than distinguishing contrasted attitudes to Sunday observance and cathedral chanting' (Introduction to *Barchester Towers*, Dent Everyman, p. x). The novel nevertheless remains a fictional tract for the times in the sense that it appraises character and motive against the important background of doctrinal differences. Trollope himself adopts a neutral tone but is clearly ironic about the political grouping at local and national level. I have already mentioned in the preceding section some notable religious protagonists, historically important Acts of Parliament regarding religion, and committees. There would be little point in going into great detail here, since any annotated edition of *Barchester Towers* is going to provide a note on, for example, the Maynooth Grant (p. 17). In his account of Arabin, Trollope undertakes a virtual potted history of the Oxford Movement (see particularly pp. 167–75) and it is true that a reader with no knowledge of the period would have little difficulty in following the parties and their basic practices merely by reading the novel. I feel, however, that it is necessary to say something of the nature of these differences here, since a fuller understanding on the part of the reader is a fuller understanding of the nature of Trollope's art.

The Low Church or Evangelical Movement within the Church of England began in the 1820s and focused on individual salvation, Sabbatarianism, good works and active reform of social evils, the latter forever associated with the name of Lord Shaftesbury. The connections with Methodism will be obvious. Diametrically opposed to this was the High Church reform group known initially as the Tractarians and later as the Oxford Movement. The chief leaders were John Keble, E. B. Pusey and John Henry Newman, and Keble's Assize Sermon in 1833 gave the Movement its impetus. The initiators published Tracts on a number of theological issues. Their original aim was to preserve the Church of England in its independence, to investigate the nature of their church, and to reject latitudinarianism. They stressed the importance of the rituals of the church, of the sacraments, of the sanctity of the priesthood as divinely ordained, and of the connection with the Church of Rome. It was the celebrated *Tract XC* by John Henry Newman which linked the thirty-nine articles (to which every Anglican clergyman had to subscribe) with Roman Catholicism. This led to a ban of the Tractarians, but in a sense it was too late. Newman himself became a Roman Catholic and, as is evident from the fictional Arabin in *Barchester Towers*, a number went over to Rome with him, leaving others sorely tempted to go. Those who remained subscribed to the rituals of Anglicanism – as we see in the High Church factions of Grantly, Arabin, Mr Harding with his intoning, and Eleanor when she becomes Mrs Arabin.

In the period covered by *Barchester Towers* there was strife within the Anglican church, hence the appropriateness of the war imagery used by Trollope. The High Church group were close to Roman Catholicism in many ways, both in terms of doctrine and ritual. In polar distinction from them were the Low Church groups with their inclinations towards Methodism and Sabbatarianism, but with the strict intention of remaining within the Anglican fold and converting the Church from within. Mrs Proudie, and of course the bishop and Slope, are manifestly of this persuasion.

The only other clergyman of note is Dr Vesey Stanhope. He is forced back into Barchester temporarily by the Low Church bishop. The Act of 1838 had given bishops the power to enforce attendance in the area, and absentee clergymen like Stanhope, who had abused their position, were less likely to get away with it after that date. (For an excellent note on the Church in *Barchester Towers*, see Robin Gilmour's introduction to the Penguin English Library Edition, pp. xxxii–iii).

3. Plot and Structure

Barchester Towers was published in three volumes in May 1857, and Trollope made a number of alterations in the text following the adverse comments of the publisher's reader. Among other things, the reader referred to 'vulgarity and exaggeration' which was likely to be 'repulsive to the reader'. He added 'plot there is none' and found the character of the Signora 'a great blot on the work'. These comments will strike the modern reader as strange, but Trollope toned down some of the language (which was in no way exceptional). His own views on fiction are clearly put in *An Autobiography*, and will serve as introduction to this section: 'I think that the highest merit which a novel can have consists in perfect delineation of character, rather than in plot, or humour, or pathos . . .' (I, 122). In a sense, the plotting of characterization, the structure of development and situation, is what Trollope is mainly concerned with in all his fiction. *Barchester Towers* is sophisticated and structurally coherent.

Trollope works using contrast and parallel and aims throughout at a balancing intensity of focus. The first chapter of volume I turns on tension and chance, ambition at a personal level (that of the archdeacon) being set against the accident of a change of government which is going to alter the disposal of church preferments. Before the end of that chapter, with expectation aroused, Trollope almost casually announces the consecration of Bishop Proudie. Yet the reader is drawn aside in the next chapter. The reason for this is the necessary integration of Mr Harding into the action through a brief but calculated retrospect on *The Warden*. Eleanor is also brought into the foreground, with John Bold somewhat arbitrarily killed off prior to the action of *Barchester Towers*. Trollope's artistic cohesion is apparent. Since the questions of the hospital appointment and who will marry Eleanor are the main pivots of interest, Trollope has set out his stall economically.

These early chapters are prologue, with an omniscient retrospect on the Proudies (not yet shown in their dual domestic/episcopal interactions) and also on Slope. Throughout this retrospect the moral tone is evident, the pace leisurely. This soon gives way to immediate action, the drama of contrasts, seen in the chapter 'A Morning Visit'. This is prelude to the war game which is to dominate the action of the novel; the archdeacon's reactions are bellicose, Mrs Proudie is installed as bishop (the 'prelatess' Trollope calls her) and Slope is initially her *aide-de-camp*. The title of the next chapter is 'War', an ironic definition of the situation in this apparently peaceful cathedral town. From now on Trollope employs the imagery of war as commentary on the progressive conflict.

Slope's sermon in the cathedral is a bold strategic move, and battle is joined on the broader ecclesiastical level. Trollope rarely reduces the narrative temperature. He maintains it by deft switches of interest. Reaction to Slope in Barchester is followed by Mr Harding's own reactions to the prospect of resuming the wardenship. This balance between the public and the personal, whether the implications are real or illusory, always marks the Trollopian perspective. But by Chapter 9 another important centre of interest is established. With the return of the Stanhopes Trollope provides us with a retrospective summary of their background and character (note that Trollope 'places' his characters socially and morally by this method) and an unequivocal projection of the Signora, who is to play such a vital part in the war and peace of Barchester.

With the exception of Mr Arabin (and more of this later) Trollope has assembled all his major characters and, having done so, he now proceeds to a social assembly so that the reader can evaluate them in interaction. 'Mrs Proudie's Reception' runs over two chapters (see the section on Scenes and Settings for further analysis) and is perhaps the richest comedy sequence in the novel. It leads directly into the forthcoming action, with the beginnings of division between Mrs Proudie and Slope over his infatuation for Madeline. There is also the eruption of the Stanhopes on to this scene, in particular Bertie and Madeline, who make their personalities immediately felt. While Madeline begins to cast her snares Bertie inadvertently humiliates Mrs Proudie and engages blithely in religious discussion and his own experiences with remarks like 'I was a Jew once myself'. This engagement is succeeded by the quiet skirmish of a letter from Slope to Mr Harding. The manoeuvre outflanks the ex-warden, while a quick burst of verbal fire from Mrs Proudie within the palace forces the surrender of the Bishop; he has no alternative but to appoint Quiverful to the warden's position.

Mr Harding retreats to Plumstead Episcopi, saddened when he hears his daughter's innuendo about her sister and Slope, though he learns that reinforcements are on the way with the archdeacon's news of the appointment of Mr Arabin to St Ewold's. This is calculated to combat the Slope/Proudie assault. The military imagery used above is a critical approximation to Trollope's own use of similar terms. But Trollope returns to the domestic front, and the parallel structure becomes increasingly clear in 'The Widow's Suitors' (Chapter 15). The irony is ever-present – Slope has offered Quiverful the wardenship and then learned casually that Eleanor Bold is rich. While Slope first thinks of marrying the widow Charlotte is laying her own plans that Bertie should do so. This chapter is evidence of Trollope's structural awareness, for the widow is to have two *failed* suitors later (Slope and Bertie), while the other 'widow' (the signora), with suitors who are moths round the light of her fascination, is to provide, through her bluntness, the one suitor that Eleanor wants, namely Arabin.

Trollope is not, as some critics maintain, careless of structure. He plots and relates meticulously. If we read this chapter carefully we shall see that Madeline's words, drawn from her personal bitterness, also relate to another major part of the plot. She observes that marriage means 'tyranny on one side, and deceit on the other'. It has been her lot, and in a sense it is the lot of the Proudies. Trollope's structural organization involves the reader at all levels or, as he puts it here, 'Our doctrine is that the reader and the author should move along together in full confidence with each other' (p. 127). Strangely, this makes for narrative tension, since the reader knows what Eleanor, for example, at this stage does not know: that her father fears she loves Slope, that the archdeacon is waxing angry on this assumption, and that Bertie is being alerted to his coming role as her suitor. The dramatic irony here is further extended in the next chapter, for 'Baby Worship' is the innocent title which covers the devious activities of Slope, and the episcopal condescension of Mrs Proudie to Mrs Quiverful. Simply, the innocence of childhood is contrasted with the experienced duplicity of man and, here, the confident authority of woman.

'Who Shall be Cock of the Walk' applies the proverbial image to the domestic struggle within the palace, but it has associations which reach into the plot. The immediate application is of course to the Slope/Mrs Proudie struggle which will demonstrate who is the real Bishop of Barchester. But there are other 'walks' which invite 'cocks' and which run throughout the novel, from the initial 'Who Will Be the New Bishop' of Chapter 1 through to who will be the Dean of Barchester, who will marry Eleanor, who will be the warden and even, on a comic level, who will succeed in Miss Thorne's quintain at Ullathorne Sports, and who will be able to match the signora. Trollope's structure, like his style, is enhanced by this allusiveness. One phrase suggests particularity *and* a wider application.

The war now switches, and Eleanor finds herself in verbal and emotional conflict with the archdeacon. This is followed by Eleanor's innocent visit to the Stanhopes, where she meets Mr Slope and where she engages in discussion with Bertie and Charlotte, unaware of their intentions regarding her. The irony of this is implicit, and makes a fitting ending to the first volume, with Slope and Bertie, so to speak, jockeying for position. The next volume opens with a first chapter devoted to Mr Arabin. This is subtle and prophetic, coming immediately after the previous moonlight scene, since the plot demands that these two, the widow and the fellow of Lazarus, should provide the denouement and the positive romance of the novel. There is the usual retrospect here to integrate Arabin into the action, and it is at once apparent that he is to be seen in conflict (religious), contrast and competition with Slope.

His introduction does more than facilitate the movement of the plot. It gives Trollope the opportunity to sketch in details of the authentic background and establish contemporary historical realism, for example the Tractarian movement and the defections to Rome. As with Chapter 1, we are aware of the local habitation and the national background, so that the opening of Volume II, like the opening of Volume I, suggests a deliberate perspective. We note that just as that first chapter confronted us with ministerial change and decision, so the wider reference which opens Volume II has Arabin's appointment to St Ewold's and its effects – the arrival of the outsider and the expectation of change. The unobtrusive parallels with Slope are also stressed. Thus the last words of this chapter are about Arabin – 'Truly he had fallen between two stools' – but they are to apply with telling irony to Slope's failure to capture either Eleanor or the Deanery.

Chapter 2 of this second volume is superbly shaped. It exposes the lack of idealism in religion, exposes Eleanor to misinterpretation, and exposes Arabin to Eleanor's sweet person. Then Trollope, whose comic art is so often in evidence in *Barchester Towers*, brings the Thornes before us in all their eccentricity, steeped in conservatism and tradition. It is a masterly control of narrative pace, since the switch to the Thornes offers its own distinctive attractions, but also arouses expectation by delay. The Thornes are lovable and rooted in the past. They are obstinate and well-meaning, essential to the plot because time and change have practically passed them by. They are presented with warmth and affection, and stand in contrast to their contemporaries who are engaged in religious controversy. Through them Trollope conveys his own pride in tradition, but he also conveys an ironic view of excessive obstinacy or bloody-mindedness. Ullathorne Court shows Trollope's fine sense of place (see the chapter on 'Scenes and Settings'), allowing a movement out from episcopal palace, country rectory or parsonage into the spacious society country house and grounds. There is, so to speak, a greater freedom of interaction being made possible by such a location, and the chapter looks forward to the 'Ullathorne Sports' chapters later.

This lengthy description is followed by the account of Mr Arabin at St Ewold's. His text and sermon are obviously meant to be contrasted with Slope's provocative first offering in the Cathedral. The parallels with Volume I continue. The morning visit there is given a dark equivalent here when Slope visits Puddingdale to wrest Quiverful's claim to the wardenship away from him. We have now come down the social scale from the Thornes through Arabin and Eleanor to the impoverished Vicar of Puddingdale who can be manipulated by this man of God in his warfare with the Bishop's wife. This Slope/Mrs Proudie confrontation now moves centre stage, and Mrs Quiverful's journey in courage and anguish, and Slope's temporary victory over Mrs Proudie, are fine dramatic strokes. Our reactions are balanced by the personalities involved, for our sympathies are with Mrs Quiverful. We do not delight in Slope's triumph, but we do enjoy Mrs Proudie's discomfort. We are aware just how good Trollope is at maintaining narrative expectation. Will Mrs Proudie win the next round from her position of strength inside the matrimonial chamber? If she does, what counter can Slope make to this? Trollope employs here the third of Wilkie Collins's maxims – 'Make 'em wait'.

Slope has initiated decision. When he writes to Eleanor (notice how letters, as in a Jane Austen novel, are employed to bring characters and readers up to date) he is inviting division within himself, for he is pursuing Eleanor materialistically and the signora romantically and, despite her deformity, sexually. It is notable too that there is nothing spiritual in his approaches. The love scene with the signora invites a comparison between her and Mrs Proudie, for both control their men although they are complete opposites in motive and character. Trollope is adept at creating contrasting atmosphere in his plot. The propitiation of the 'widow' (Slope with Madeline) is quickly followed by the continuing persecution of the widow (the archdeacon, his wife as milder protagonist, and Eleanor). This is preparatory to 'A Serious Interview' (Chapter 19) over which the darker side of Trollope's irony plays. It is superbly direct and movingly dramatic. The archdeacon blunders, but he does so from a reasonable assumption. Eleanor's letter from Slope seems to be confirmation of her guilt, and her own obstinacy compounds the error. The irony covers the involvement of Arabin. Here we penetrate to the heart of Trollope's psychological matter, for Eleanor's reactions are human, biased, completely convincing.

In the next chapter Trollope sharpens the focus of the reader's sympathy by returning to Arabin. Just as Eleanor does not know her own mind or, more accurately, her own emotions, so 'Mr Arabin was now in love with Mrs Bold, though ignorant of the fact himself'. The conversation between Arabin and Eleanor is a confrontation, remarkable for its sensitivity, which brings about a not altogether unpredictable development. When Eleanor upbraids Arabin she does not draw from him the declaration we might have expected, but an ill-considered request for an assurance that Eleanor is not in love with Slope and that she is not going to marry him. It shows Arabin's inexperience with women (the contrast with Slope is implicit), but Eleanor 'knew that it all meant love'.

The end of Chapter 12 finds Eleanor and Arabin inwardly close to each other but outwardly as far apart as ever. And it is at this stage that Trollope reproduces an earlier situation. Just as it took some time for the old bishop to die, so now it takes some time for the old dean to die, and narrative tension accumulates. There is room for manoeuvre, sycophancy, publicity, canvassing as Slope, in his bid for the deanery, takes on the High Church (and Mrs Proudie) in order to win this plum. In Trollope's own war imagery, a new campaign opens. Slope appears to get the bishop on his side, but has to make the important concession that Mrs Proudie's nominee, Quiverful, shall have the hospital. The tensions, the balances, are always taking the strain, for Slope is putting opportunist promotion before the possibility of Eleanor's hand in marriage.

But other ambitions are also being promoted. Although Slope is to go with the Stanhopes and Eleanor to Ullathorne, neither Slope nor Eleanor knows that Charlotte is working towards her own determination to get Bertie into the right position, and frame of mind, to propose to Eleanor. Meanwhile, knowing of Slope's ambitions to be dean, Mrs Proudie determines that he will not be the bishop's chaplain for much longer. A classical reference ironically underlines Mrs Proudie's Christian charity. We are told that she was 'the Medea of Barchester; she had no idea of not eating Mr Slope . . . she would pick him to the very last bone'. But an even more telling classical analogy – 'Dr Gwynne was the *deus ex machina* who was to come down upon the Barchester stage' – ends Volume II on a high and unexpected note with the idea that Mr Harding may be offered the deanery. Trollope was greatly interested in seventeenth-century drama. Here we see his sense of dramatic irony as the gods (in Oxford) determine the fate of man, but in *Barchester Towers* it is comic rather than tragic art.

The third volume opens with one of the most important scene settings in the whole novel. The initial concentration is on Slope, triumphant at being invited to Ullathorne (is it prophetic of a forthcoming temporal or spiritual invitation?). This is of course ironic, for it is on this day that he is to receive both metaphorical blows to his pride and physical blows to his person. Linked to the irony is a satirical account (though not unkind) of the guests and the gradations of class distinction, seen in the niceties of who is placed where and when. The preparations and the waiting provide much comedy before the humorous interactions, but the word 'sports' in the titles of three chapters sufficiently indicates Trollope's own attitude of amusement. Having one's face slapped is a kind of sport (though not for Slope or Eleanor), while Trollope's reference to 'acts' conveys the genuine dramatic, or even melodramatic flavour.

In one way Trollope is doing what he so often likes to do, that is, playfully reminding us by his attitudes and perspective that we are reading fiction, that these scenes of social entertainment for the guests are dramatic entertainment for *his* guests, the readers. This is highlighted further in the lists of guests, a mock-heroic parody of the lists of gods in an epic poem. Eleanor gets off to a good start in the serious matter of her life: she enlightens her relieved father about her real feelings for Slope. The second phase is shared by Mrs Proudie and Lady De Courcy on the one hand and the signora on the other. E. M. Forster's motif of 'only connect' is Trollope's structural method. As we see from the heading to Chapter 4, 'The Bishop Breakfasts, and the Dean Dies', the small alliterative antithesis connects the supremely important (for some) with the commonplace and trivial. But Trollope's simple chapter headings are sometimes, like George Eliot's chapter mottoes, a subtle covering for what is occurring at a deeper level. In this chapter the signora interrogates Arabin, and in doing so proves to herself that she is right about the state of his feelings for Eleanor. She observes idly, 'I'll do all in my power to make up the match,' and later a positive impulse towards this end moves her to do so after she has waited to see that Bertie has failed.

The class interaction between Lookalofts and Greenacres maintains the comic flow on a different level, while the second Act of the Ullathorne Sports sees Eleanor box Slope's ear. From now on the action gathers narrative pace and the omnipresent irony accompanies it. Eleanor confides Slope's infamy to Charlotte, sublimely unaware of Charlotte's infamy to her in manoeuvring Bertie to a proposal. The third act of what Trollope calls a 'melodrama' has the farce of Bertie's indolent approach and his confiding of Charlotte's plan to Eleanor, and the latter's anger that takes her into 'the last act' of the day's performance. Chapter 9 sees the appointment of the Quiverfuls confirmed while their patroness shows her vulgarity before Dr Gwynne. The *Jupiter* 'just now five years since' had seen fit to pronounce on Mr Harding's holding the sinecure at Hiram's Hospital, and now takes up the cudgels on Slope's behalf as he lays claim to the deanery.

This focus on the various levels of interactions is a sharp one, but even sharper is the verisimilitude of Eleanor's reactions of disgust to her declared suitors. She has no idea that Madeline has plans for her that will change her life, and she gets the message at the end of the chapter saying that the signora wishes to see her. Before Eleanor calls we have a further incisive insight into the Stanhopes in 'The Stanhopes at Home', which conveys the severity of Dr Stanhope, the resilience of Charlotte and the oblivious talent for caricature of Bertie. Madeline's influence on Eleanor and the quality of the exchanges between them, is one of the finest scenes in the novel. Though lighter in texture, it may be compared with the scene between Rosamond and Dorothea in George Eliot's *Middlemarch* where Rosamond performs the one morally generous action of her life in telling Dorothea that Will loves her (Dorothea). Madeline undertakes a like function with commendable bluntness, and we feel her own sense of deprivation ('What would I not give to be loved in such a way by such a man, that is, if I were an object fit for any man to love.')

Trollope, as we have seen, works with parallel and contrast always in mind. Chapter 12 underlines the sincerity of the previous chapter by showing Madeline ruthlessly, even cruelly, baiting Slope over her proposal to Eleanor. Trollope is now emphasizing the humiliation of Slope with Mr Harding's being offered the deanery and, more dramatically, Harding's determination to refuse it, to the discomfort of the archdeacon. The contrast also includes the archdeacon's worldliness seen against Mr Harding's humility *and* integrity. With an intuitive eye on the expectations of his readers, Trollope now switches the narrative adroitly back to Eleanor. In one of the finest proposal scenes in fiction Eleanor accepts Mr Arabin. I say proposal scenes, but in fact very few words of love are used. Yet the emotions, the sympathetic and corresponding, if unvoiced, feelings between the lovers are described explicitly through consciousness and commentary. Eleanor's revelation of the news to her father is moving, Mr Harding's revelation of Eleanor's engagement to the archdeacon humorous, with the father enjoying the joke of the archdeacon's ignorance which at one time he shared. Harding, not Dr Gwynne, proves to be a quietly cunning *deus ex machina* in his proposal to get Arabin made dean.

Parallel and contrast run through to the end. Slope goes, Arabin enters upon his new duties. There is one projection here which was altered later in the sequence. Trollope writes of Bishop Proudie that he 'never again aspired to disobey, or seemed even to wish for autocratic diocesan authority'. He does disobey, in revolt against his wife's domination, as we see in *The Last Chronicle*. It is obvious from this that Trollope had not fully considered the future of the series at this stage (ten years separate *Barchester Towers* and *The Last Chronicle*). Curiously, two sentences later, Trollope continues with 'the bishop had no reason to apprehend that he would be speedily visited with the sorrows of a widower's life'. The irony in *The Last Chronicle* is that those projected sorrows become a kind of muted joy. Lastly, the imagery of war reaches its conclusion too, for the battles have been won. Eleanor the wife acquires a 'few high church vagaries', but the author continues to assert his own neutrality in things ecclesiastical.

Clearly, plot control and a careful organization of narrative tensions constitute an important aspect of Trollope's method in *Barchester Towers*. The adroit use of contrast and parallel make it a richly satisfying experience. Like so many other novelists of his time, Trollope subscribes to the need for a happy ending, that Victorian anodyne for the ills of reality. *Barchester Towers* ends with Slope renewing the chase for a widow in the distance as compensation for the one he lost in the foreground. And tying all the ends together is the unifying voice of the author. It is heard most often in its ironic appraisal of character and situation and in its evaluation of the contrasts and parallels indicated above. *Barchester Towers* is not loosely or haphazardly constructed; it is taut, with its division of narrative interests. The reader feels for Harding, Eleanor and Arabin, and responds angrily or critically to the archdeacon, Slope and Mrs Proudie. But Trollope also cultivates a middle way, and is perhaps ambivalent towards Madeline, Bertie, Charlotte, and even the bishop. His perspective reflects, over this comparatively small social area, the variety of human nature and of human responses. His characters are viewed from a moral perspective, but presented with convincing psychological fullness.

4. Characters and Themes

Characters and themes, as in most novels, are interrelated in *Barchester Towers*, and I intend here to look at the relationship between the two. The encapsulation of character traits in the novel is seen against the spectrum of moral, social and spiritual values. Trollope represents characters typical of his time and of a particular part of England who belong, in the main, to the Church or have connections with it.

Septimus Harding

Let us first of all take the common link with *The Warden*, Septimus Harding. He passes through *Barchester Towers* certainly as one of the mainsprings of the action (the question of the hospital is still to be settled) and on into *The Last Chronicle*, where he dies peacefully in old age. There is little doubt that for the 'neutral' Trollope he represents the ideal clergyman. There is little doubt, also, that he is linked to several Trollopian themes which are clearly related, the main ones being those of humility and integrity.

The archdeacon is worldly, priding himself on a gentlemanly, cultivated standard of living (he is the old bishop's son). His father-in-law, Mr Harding, has always been something of an embarrassment to him, since he is other-worldly and, most important of all, unaggressive, wishing to be left to care for his old men, but not prepared to wage all-out war in view of the doubts concerning his right to a comfortable living. We remember the pressures brought to bear on Mr Harding in *The Warden* by the archdeacon, and how the latter's visit to the bedesmen embarrassed the warden by its loud, insensitive condescension. Harding is only of the archdeacon's world because his eldest daughter married into it. His is an essentially *simple* nature, and here that is a term of praise rather than of limitation. His church music is sacred to him and in his music practising, oblivious to others, he is at once endearing and eccentric. He loves innocently, spiritually, movingly, and we remember in *The Warden* the implicit fullness of love between himself and the old bishop. He represents civilized Christian practice and dedication without benefit of dogma. In *Barchester Towers* he no longer has his old men, or the bishop, and his cares are family ones, though he takes a public blow when Slope makes his calculated attack on, among other things, church music, in his first sermon in the cathedral. It seems that in Harding's middle to late life he is doomed to suffer. He is nearly convinced that Eleanor will marry Slope. He tries to reason with himself to be reconciled to it if she does so. He knows that he would like to be warden again, but he is disconcerted – or rather, deeply worried and affronted – by the conditions Slope affects to attach to his acceptance. When he is offered the deanery he has the self-honesty (which is synonymous with integrity) to wish to turn it down despite the pressure he is put under by his son-in-law.

Here Trollope's characterization takes on a new subtlety, for Harding has an inherent weakness when he is forced into the position of being something of a public figure. He prefers anonymity, unlike the archdeacon, who is loud and often abrasive. Harding's refusal of the deanery can, therefore, be seen in two ways, and I suspect that there is both integrity and weakness in his wish to reject it. When the archdeacon asks him to consider his position he does so to very good effect, for he has the delightful, and for him cunning, idea of having Arabin take his place as dean. For those of us who have read *The Warden* this somewhat sly quality (it means he gets his own way) is not surprising. He also has a degree of obstinacy (Eleanor is like her father in this way). Moreover, Harding retreats from the world (his silent playing of music is a symptom of this) when the emotional pressures get too much for him. His music is his self-protection and a source of his serenity. The breath of the world sometimes blows too strongly for Harding, but he has the kind of self-knowledge that I would equate with integrity. He knows himself well enough to know what he cannot do.

Harding is portrayed in contrast to the archdeacon, nowhere more clearly than in the first chapter where the question of integrity is directly involved. The archdeacon is deeply concerned about his father's approaching death, but he is a practical opportunist who has to act decisively if he is to succeed to his father's position. He has qualms of conscience about the nature of this immediate ambition. Harding is oppressed by constant watching over the dying man, but his love and feeling for his old friend are obvious. Just before the bishop dies we are told of Harding and the archdeacon that as 'they stood there pressing each other's hands, the tears rolled freely down their cheeks' (p. 4). This is typical of Harding's (usually inward) emotional nature, but quite untypical of the archdeacon, who nearly always remembers that he is a public man. Trollope is generally careful to preserve a more public image of man, though Harding is seen frequently from within because of the author's sympathetic identification with him. The emphasis on the archdeacon's clerical and social roles militates against intimacy.

When the archdeacon recovers himself here the action is swift. Harding feels himself 'very much like an errand-boy' when he is told to send the telegram (p. 6) which, the archdeacon hopes, will be in time to secure his own preferment as bishop. Here we see the positive strengths of Trollope's thematic characterization. Harding has integrity and, by his own lights, so has the archdeacon. But whereas the archdeacon does not acknowledge weakness or question deeply his own motives, Harding is aware of his weaknesses and continually questions himself.

Linked to Harding's integrity is his humility, a quality which is not conspicuously present in the archdeacon. In social and family interaction, specifically with Slope and the archdeacon, Harding's humility means that he will put up with much, rather than hit back. But Harding is no worm and he puts up a resistance when the provocations and pressures become too strong. His earlier resignation of the wardenship and his undertaking the 'small parish of St Cuthbert's' shows an obstinacy and determination which are wholly commendable (in the Trollopian and moral sense). There is even an indication of inner strength, which balances any weakness, in his settling over a shop in the High Street, rather than being persuaded to stay with his younger daughter, now widowed. His vanity, as Trollope tells us, is confined to his church music, while his dedication to his old men has continued without official blessing, another mark of his integrity.

He is now faced, in *Barchester Towers*, with the pressures of uncertainty over his appointment to the hospital and over Eleanor's relationship with Slope, the latter situation making him tremulous. It is an indication of Trollope's consistency in presenting character that although Mr Harding is absent from much of the action of the novel, when he does appear we can anticipate how he will behave – with the single exception of his contriving the deanery for Arabin. That his integrity and humility represent for Trollope the right moral attitude is clear from the fifth chapter of the first volume, 'A Morning Visit'. While the questions of Sabbath schools, Sunday trains and 'the palatial dilapidations' are the main areas of controversy, Harding says little. He is overcome by the weight of the verbal onslaught, but he is quick to perceive the unethical behaviour of Mrs Proudie:

> Mr Harding had never been so hard pressed in his life. He felt that he ought to rebuke the lady for presuming so to talk to a gentleman and a clergyman many years her senior; but he recoiled from the idea of scolding the bishop's wife, in the

bishop's presence, on his first visit to the palace; moreover, to tell the truth, he was somewhat afraid of her. (p. 35)

This goes a long way towards establishing the kind of man Harding is: well-bred, uncertain, apprehensive, honest, acting with integrity, fundamentally a man of judgement and sensitivity. If anyone is to speak to him about official duties he feels that it should be the bishop, and not the bishop's wife. The kind of confrontation we see in the scene above is a favourite one with Trollope (see Mr Crawley's and Dr Tempest's response to Mrs Proudie's assumption of authority in *The Last Chronicle*). Here Trollope cleverly follows Harding's silence with Harding's action, which is an effective way of putting Mrs Proudie down. He takes his leave of her by shaking her hand and telling her (in relation to 'sabbath travelling') to 'come to St Cuthbert's some Sunday, and I will preach you a sermon on that subject' (p. 36).

Another major aspect of Harding's character is tolerance, and again it is seen in contrast to the intolerance of others, such as the archdeacon and Slope. Harding's reaction to the scene we have just discussed is merely to observe that he cannot see himself liking Mrs Proudie and Slope, but he is cautious about the bishop and reserves his judgement. He begins to protect himself against their intrusion into his life, expressing the view that Eleanor need not visit the palace. The seeds of his own insecurity have been sown during the visit and they sprout with Slope's sermon. Harding, who dislikes even the faintest lights of publicity, finds himself publicly, as well as personally, implicated by Slope's criticisms. Always susceptible and vulnerable, he finds himself the cynosure of controversy with Slope's attack on 'the meretricious charms of melody' (p. 45). His reactions are poignantly described. He 'crept forth solitary and unhappy . . . Was he again to be disturbed? was his whole life to be shown up as a useless sham a second time?' (p. 48). Trollope provides his own comment, placing Harding in perspective against the worldly by saying: 'Doubting himself was Mr Harding's weakness. It is not, however, the usual fault of his order' (p. 48). This could be read as an authorial dig at the archdeacon.

Harding continues to exemplify moderation in the debate, urging that Slope should not be silenced 'unless he preached false doctrine' (p. 50). Again we are made aware of some subtlety in the presentation, for Harding is, I think, astute enough to feel that Slope may condemn himself out of his own mouth. Mr Harding's eye for other people's motives is not as naïve as it may appear. After Slope has visited Eleanor and praised her father, Mr Harding sees enough, though 'it was not his practice to say much evil of anyone' (p. 55), to suspect Slope's motives. He is right, but generally his natural tolerance takes on a trusting quality. Before his interview with Slope he displays a certain naïveté in his assurance that he will resume the wardenship. He concedes the justice of a reduced salary, and jokes about the idea of a matron and who will manage her. Yet his pride is already making him feel that he 'should never go there, if it were necessary that my doing so should be the subject of a request to Mr Slope' (p. 59), his presentiments here showing a degree of intuition. Mr Harding is far from being a simple character; he is a study in reticence, but that reticence is occasionally raised to show us the strength of the inner man.

I have said that he is vulnerable (a quality he shares with his daughter Eleanor and also with Arabin). He is flustered by the bishop's approach to him, and 'oppressed and annoyed' (p. 91) at the thought of having to discuss the details of his return to the hospital with Slope. The latter's letter summoning him to an interview strikes the wrong note, and Harding is so greatly moved before he sees him that he is not in a fit emotional condition to deal with the wily manoeuvres of the ambitious chaplain. He is kept waiting, Slope's psychological ploy to make him feel uneasy; he suffers Slope's sarcasm, but is angered by a smile which is insulting to the late bishop. Yet again we are made aware of Harding's resources. Although angry and, in part, humiliated, he has the perspicacity to ask the one question which Slope cannot answer: 'But if I accept the appointment, and yet disagree with the bishop, what then?' (p. 100). He nearly circumvents Slope by saying that he intends to see the bishop. His vulnerability is well in evidence. He has been wounded by Slope's language about 'rubbish' and by the false sense it gives rise to that his life has been wasted. He soon encounters the additional fear that Eleanor has been influenced by Slope. His dependence on her is made explicit, for 'he could not afford to be cut off from the one whose sympathy was of the most value to him' (p. 107). With this fear, and the uncompromising attitude of the archdeacon towards the supposedly compromised Eleanor, Harding copes as best he can with quiet Christian fortitude. Unbeknown to himself, he is now a pawn in the Mrs Proudie–Slope power struggle.

Harding is also caught up in the mutually destructive interaction between the archdeacon and Eleanor, his sympathies and doubts being with his daughter, while he has to endure the suspicions and bias of the archdeacon. Harding's sense of fairness – his integrity again – forces him, unhappily, to tolerate whatever he fears may occur. He is, as we have seen in *The Warden*, not lacking in moral courage, and he determines to 'get over his aversion (to Slope) as best he could' (pp. 150–51).

Trollope goes on to tell us that 'Mr Harding was by no means a perfect character. In his indecision, his weakness, his proneness to be led by others, his want of self-confidence, he was very far from being perfect . . . in his charity he did not hate the chaplain as the archdeacon did, and as we do' (p. 151). It is a striking statement, further evidence of what I have chosen to call the man's integrity. We accept the authorial bias as our own, but his very imperfections make us warm to Harding for they make us aware of his humaneness and his charitable nature.

Trollope's irony ensures that, when Slope learns of Eleanor's portion, Mr Harding now has his past enemy as his present ally over the wardenship. Harding's influence on the action, despite his absence from it, is now decisive for, although Mrs Proudie has lost the initial round over the appointment, it is certain that she will ultimately win the contest. This means that Harding will lose and Slope will be put down. During this interaction Quiverful himself pays tribute to Harding's integrity, for he so respects him that he will not accept the wardenship despite the pressures of his wife and their poverty unless he knows that Harding has positively refused it. Meanwhile Harding continues to display great moral courage as he finds himself trapped between Eleanor and the archdeacon. His own obstinacy comes to the fore, and he defends Eleanor by saying that if she marries Slope 'I shall certainly not think that she disgraces herself' (p. 255). Trollope, as commentator, bemoans the fact that Harding keeps quiet and does not ask Eleanor about her intentions with regard to Slope. But it is completely in character that he should refrain, for his fears are much too strong and he puts off having them confirmed. When he sees Slope's letter to Eleanor, Harding is now certain in his own mind that Eleanor must have encouraged Slope. As Trollope puts it, the 'father's spirits sank within him as he felt that he could not acquit her' (p. 265). Mr Harding's fundamental error about Eleanor might be construed as a weakness of judgement, but it has the effect of rounding the character more completely. In his delicacy and anxiety he holds back, but if he had brought himself to speak 'one word would have cleared up everything' (p. 266). Life hinges on such might-have-beens, and Harding's reactions here are so natural that they enhance the realism of his portrait. Trollope calls him a 'foolish, weak, loving man' (p. 266), and by doing so binds us all to him.

Suddenly Harding's burden is lightened when Eleanor says to him at Ullathorne that Slope is 'a horrid odious man' (p. 347), though he has to suffer Eleanor's indignant castigation of his suspicions. As always with Harding, his priorities are the human ones, and we are told that he was 'so indifferent as to the loss of the hospital, so thankful for the recovery of his daughter' (p. 349).

He remains ignorant of the feelings of Eleanor and Arabin for each other (as, indeed, do they), and it is only after Eleanor returns home from Ullathorne, and learns of Quiverful's appointment to the hospital, that she tells her father of Slope's proposal. Relieved by Eleanor's rejection of her unwelcome suitor, he makes light of Quiverful becoming warden. He is more concerned over the death of the dean (ironically so, in view of the invitation which will be extended to him). He admits that once the hospital attracted publicity again 'I thoroughly wished to be rid of it' (p. 428), and says that his chief hope is for peace and quiet. Events once more overtake him. When he is offered the deanery he knows that it will lead to restlessness, disagreement, all the effects attendant upon being in the public eye, but he has the character to stand up to the archdeacon by proposing to reject it. He does this with courage, modesty, and perhaps a little self-interest, saying 'I do not find myself fit for new duties' (p. 455). Again we are aware of the subtle combination of self-interest and integrity. Harding's clear-sightedness and self-awareness enable him to tell his daughter that 'I want the force of character which might enable me to stand against the spirit of the times' (p. 456). There is a clever underlining of a character trait here. Harding regards himself as a failed warden, not in the Christian sense of his care for the old men, but because he held a sinecure. He is not prepared to make the same mistake again. He searches for a way out and, with the revelation of Eleanor's love for Arabin, finds it to hand. The way he puts forward the scheme to have Arabin made dean is a masterstroke of timing. It is as if those unwelcome worldly experiences have equipped him with a kind of cunning.

His final action is generous, kind, understanding, thoughtful as he conducts Mr Quiverful round his hospital. Before that with 'eyes brim full of tears' (p. 491) he has made his future son-in-law acquainted with his good fortune. Typically, rather than offend, he gives up his lodgings in the High Street. With covert irony Trollope observes 'What could a weak old man do but yield?' (p. 491). But the weak old man makes sure that the good he intended is achieved. By accompanying the new warden Harding ensures that Quiverful will be treated with respect. The last words of the novel underline the moral importance attached to Harding by Trollope. He writes of him 'as a good man without guile, believing humbly in the religion which he has striven to teach, and guided by the precepts which he has striven to learn' (p. 499). But this ideal never departs from credibility in his presentation; the goodness never cloys because the weaknesses common to us all are clearly there.

*

I have attempted to show how Mr Harding, in his interaction with other characters in the novel, is affected by one of its major themes, that of power. Power is crucial here, and is given varied emphasis. That Trollope is concerned with the dominance of power is clear from the first chapter of the novel, with the death of the bishop, the archdeacon's self-interest, and the delightfully ironic way the outgoing prime minister is seen to pass the minor matter of conferring a bishopric on to his successor in between the priority attractions of the Newmarket list and a French novel.

In Barchester, the bishop, elevated to power, has virtually none, since his wife and Slope have arrogated it to themselves. It is part of the irony that Mr Harding and Mr Quiverful do not strive; others strive for them for their own ends. The balance of power within the palace provides one of the main dramatic pivots in the novel. Slope, as protégé-turned-usurper, is conscious of the new opportunities provided by the bishop's position, and conscious, also, of the shackles which he must throw off in order to achieve permanent security and power. The odds are loaded against him in the long run. Mrs Proudie is flesh of the bishop's flesh, the prelatess who intends to maintain and exert power through patronage. It is to Obadiah Slope, and his ambitious schemes for self-advancement, that we now turn.

Mr Slope

At first sight Slope appears to be merely caricature, but there is more to him than that. He represents the unctuous, persuasive, hypocritical opportunist intent on power. He has to win total influence over the bishop, gain preferment or take up an outside position. He is forced to do the last, but only with a struggle after which he is finally compelled to leave gracelessly. Initially, he has to fight anyway if he wants to be more than merely Mrs Proudie's protégé. Slope, however, does his homework; he knows that power is built on the foundations of a knowledge of its object plus the opportunism of the moment.

Trollope prepares us for the kind of man Slope is in the fourth chapter of the first volume, and then shows him in action in the next chapter, 'with his catalogue of grievances' in a brilliant cross-talk act with Mrs Proudie and the bishop (p. 35). His preaching in the cathedral marks the public opening of hostilities, for 'it was immediately evident that the good clergy of Barchester were to have a lesson' (p. 43). The attack on High-Church practice certainly accords with the views of his patroness, but Trollope emphasizes that no one 'could mistake him for a fool or a coward' (p. 43). Indeed Trollope, who goes to some pains to describe Slope in physically unflattering terms, never criticizes him for lack of nerve.

Slope has a way, a kind of power, with women. Trollope finds an historical analogy by way of illustration when he observes that 'Wilkes was most fortunate as a lover: and the damp, sandy-haired, saucer-eyed, red-fisted Mr Slope was powerful only over the female breast' (p. 49). In his attempts to assume power Slope employs a dual approach. Knowing at this stage that he has the support of Mrs Proudie, he supports Quiverful's appointment over Harding's. His first brush with the latter shows just how determined Slope is to assert his will. His letter to Harding reveals, however, the nature of his duality. He is able to oil the wheels of power by unctuous flattery when he is in the presence of women, whether they have sensuality, money, or both. With Harding, on the other hand, he is intent on commanding authority. He is calculating beyond measure, but lacks the far-sightedness to estimate the repercussions. His handling of Harding is unequivocal, rude, ill-bred, insensitive and calculated to provoke, particularly when he allows himself that smile in denigration of the dead bishop, Harding's old friend. Slope's cunning is evident. He wishes to make sure that Harding will be moved to reject the wardenship because of the attendant conditions. He employs emotive language when he talks of 'carting away the useless rubbish of past centuries'. 'Work is now required from every man who receives wages' (p. 99) he adds pointedly, which ensures Harding's opposition and, at the same time, humiliates him.

Shortly after Slope has committed himself to this bullying course he learns from Quiverful that Eleanor is an heiress (note the irony again), and this just after he has told Quiverful that 'Mr Harding did positively refuse it' (p. 118) with all the power of the bishop's representative or, as he feels in his own mind, the voice of the bishop himself. Motivating Slope's ambition is the need for security and the greed for affluence which will help to make him the gentleman which he is not. Now, couched in the imagery of the war he has helped to initiate, he has to change his tactics, realizing that it will be 'much more easy for him to gain the daughter if he did all in his power to forward the father's views' (p. 119). He joins in the baby worship, pays Eleanor compliments, misrepresents her father's reactions even to the extent of wilfully misquoting him, and then preens himself as the champion of her father's cause: 'I am truly anxious for your father's welfare – for his and for your own' (p.137). Slope reads Eleanor's hesitancy about him, but such is his invidious influence that, with Mary Bold's advice, Eleanor is moved to give him the benefit of the doubt.

Slope's interview with Eleanor leads him to his direct confrontation with Mrs Proudie. The latter's daughters, and particularly Olivia, once pursued and now discarded by Slope, support her in her condemnation of Slope's impudence. Mrs Proudie does not pull her verbal punches and the archdeacon sees through his manoeuvres, but as Trollope observes at the end of Chapter 18, 'Mr Slope is certainly becoming of some importance in Barchester' (p. 153). Having been expressly warned by Mrs Proudie over his conduct with regard to the signora, he flouts convention and worships at her couch, while still keeping Eleanor well within his sights. Bertie Stanhope sees through him and reveals to Eleanor that he is false. Slope proceeds to demonstrate his falsity on his next visit to Quiverful.

Slope has learned that one of the secrets of exercising power is to make others believe that they are wrong. He brings moral blackmail to bear upon Quiverful. He plays on Quiverful's decency and the man's respect for Harding's decency. Such is Slope's command of the easy phrase – even to the point of an apparently frank admission of his own errors – that he makes Quiverful feel guilty, persuades him to renounce any claim to the wardenship, and misleads him with the promise that the bishop has other offers within his gift. Slope, the ecclesiastical salesman, has withdrawn his own special offer on the promise that others will follow.

But although exercise of power has corrupted Slope, he has not succeeded in conning Mrs Quiverful. That lady's perpetual battle with survival moves her to see Mrs Proudie. Slope now has too many enemies to succeed in either rebellion or war. But he continues with unfailing determination and faith in himself to pursue his intrigues, whether of an amorous nature with the signora, or of a materialistic one, as with Eleanor. When Slope wins a fleeting victory over Mrs Proudie he 'turned on the vanquished lady a look of triumph which she never forgot and never forgave' (p. 234). In a bid to dominate completely, he tries to ensure that the bishop is got away from under the immediate wifely influence.

During this brief period of illusory power Slope is quick to acquaint Eleanor with what he has done on her father's behalf. He is also quick to get himself once more into the signora's presence, and Trollope defines this division of interests antithetically when he observes 'Mr Slope was pursuing Mrs Bold in obedience to his better instincts, and the signora in obedience to his worser' (p. 241). It is a neat condemnation, implying not only that Eleanor is a worthier object of pursuit, but also that material motives for such a chase might be more commendable than sensual ones. Slope is, however, teased and deflated by the signora. The infatuated man who keeps the widow Bold's £1000 constantly in his mind is guilty of gross hypocrisy: 'Oh, Madeline!' said he, 'tell me that you love me – do you – do you love me?' (p. 252).

The greatest undermining factor in Slope's pursuit of power is his lack of any self-critical appraisal. Oily and persuasive, he never tries to see himself through the eyes of others, and this is his downfall. Of all the characters who crave power in this novel, only Madeline knows herself, as well as others, through and through. The archdeacon is forced, in the end, to recognize his own wrong-headed prejudices. Slope cannot see that he is an object of amusement and contempt to Madeline. He cannot see that any response Eleanor makes to him (before she boxes his ears) derives primarily from concern for her father. Nor does he clearly see, as I have indicated earlier, that he has no hope of defeating Mrs Proudie in the long term. So blinkered is he to moral decency that he does not recognize that his attempts to canvass support for election as dean are ill-judged, cheap, and doomed to failure. By propositioning Tom Towers he has almost ensured that he will not get the job.

Slope's movement towards power is motivated by greed and ambition. Trollope is at pains to tell us that he is not a gentleman, and since gentlemanly behaviour and rightness of conduct are also Trollopian themes (indeed, ideals) we must consider his characterization in the light of these qualities. Slope is not well-born; he achieves the chaplaincy through the patronage of Mrs Proudie. His letter to Eleanor, which so upsets Mr Harding and the archdeacon, shows the complacency and vulgarity of the man. Such is his insensitivity that a snub or passing coldness cannot affect his *amour propre*. Trollope defends Eleanor's response to Slope by saying that she thought of him as her father did but 'she did not think it necessary to apologize for, or condemn, or even allude to the vulgarity of the man's tone which arose, as does all vulgarity, from ignorance' (p. 265). Slope's vulgarity is a serious hindrance to his attaining power whether of the romantic, secular or ecclesiastical variety. He offends against good taste and the manners of good society. We may have more than a sneaking sympathy for the outsider, which he is, but the thematic moral constant in a Trollope novel is a condemnation of over-assertiveness, of unpardonable smugness, of vanity, and, particularly, of promoting self-interest to the exclusion of others' feelings. Slope's vulgarity and arrogance get him more than a box on the ear; after Eleanor's blow (we admire his resilience) his persistence and ambition continue undeterred, and he accosts the bishop and Dr Gwynne, but is coldly rebuffed by them. The bishop *does* feel that Slope might be dean as he begins to think it through, mainly because he wants to be rid of Slope in a covert way, since he hates the thought of continuing friction with his wife which can only lead to his being regularly defeated.

Slope now pursues another path to power through written emollients. Both Sir Nicholas Fitzwhiggin and Tom Towers get letters, but inside the palace the news of his ambitions stirs Mrs Proudie's wrath. While the old dean lingers on, Slope makes his advance to Eleanor. His self-conceit is remarkable. We are told that on the journey to Ullathorne 'Mr Slope's civility had been more than ordinarily greasy' (p. 343), while his proposal is put in language which is certainly hypocritical, in view of his avowals to the signora – 'I love you with the truest affection which man can bear to woman' (p. 383) – with a fluency induced by champagne. As we have seen, Slope quickly overcomes his 'deep agony of soul' (p. 386) though his pride, for the first time in the novel, is wounded and he is indeed made angry.

He fails to get the deanery despite the propagandist puff of Tom Towers, is humiliated at the hands of the signora and by the knowledge that 'Mrs Proudie had checkmated him' (p. 482) but, ever alert to other areas into which he can channel his ambition, he soon gets a widow, his own church, and a respectable reputation. His last battle with Mrs Proudie shows him emerging with some dignity from the vituperation of the woman: 'May God forgive you, madam, for the manner in which you have treated me' (p. 486). He finds his own niche of power and, doubtless, the material prosperity which he has always craved. Slope may verge on caricature at times, for the authorial voice is disposed, in no uncertain terms, against him but, in the end, he is not subdued. Mrs Proudie's domestic and physical demise awaits *The Last Chronicle*.

Mrs Proudie

Mrs Proudie is power-conscious in every sense. Like Slope, she is far from being caricature, though it must be acknowledged that she is given greater depth and consistency in *The Last Chronicle*. After a long introduction to the bishop, Trollope adopts an ironic stance towards Mrs Proudie, saying that it 'is not my intention to breathe a word against Mrs Proudie' but, he adds tellingly, 'she rules supreme over her titular lord, and rules with a rod of iron . . . the bishop is henpecked' (p. 19). A comparable directness of language characterizes Mrs Proudie's own utterances, which are forthright, frequently outspoken, and often downright rude. She is described as despotic, and she certainly covets power. Even as early in the novel as Chapter 3, Mrs Proudie is presented as a tyrant to the servants, given to the 'strict observance of Sabbatarian rule', watching over both with 'the eyes of Argus' (p. 21). In the way in which she assumes power as 'prelatess' she is subtly presented by Trollope.

She has ostensibly taken Slope under her spiritual and temporal wings, but her attitude towards him is condescending and patronizing. She has been completely blind to his courtship of her daughter Olivia. Mrs Proudie is a woman of powerful feelings who has succeeded in channelling them into her husband's career. However, these feelings become less controllable in her confrontation with Slope.

As long as Dr Proudie is influenced by her alone, all is well in the palace. But when Slope threatens to usurp her rule, she turns against him. Her anger towards the man is compounded by sexual jealousy of the signora, on whom Slope dotes, although Mrs Proudie is never consciously made aware of these feelings. Her response to being effectively scorned by Slope suggests, indirectly, that she has been sublimating her own sexual attraction for him into supporting his ambition.

The first evidence of jealousy is seen at her party reception. Mrs Proudie has a formidable formality about her before this. She calls her husband 'bishop' and 'my lord', and refers disparagingly to 'play-acting' (she means the way Mr Harding sings the litany). At her reception she shows clearly her lust for power with an arrogance of manner which here, and later, is to embarrass her husband. She is rigid in her attitude to social class and etiquette and is described as 'measuring out the quantity of her favours to the quality of her guests' (p. 80). She is unsuccessful in patronizing Madeline, for whenever she speaks to her 'the lady replied by speaking to Mr Slope' (p. 84). There follows the terrible humiliation of the accident to her lace train. It is a kind of sexual humiliation, since Madeline laughs and looks Mrs Proudie full in the face. She rages when Slope disobeys her by taking refreshments to the signora and her language hardly becomes her new-found status. The repressed sexuality is unleashed, and she refers to Madeline as 'a painted Jezebel' adding 'I'd lame her if she belonged to me' (p. 94). This kind of reaction shows not only Mrs Proudie's fury, but also her inherent vulnerability. She is touchy, proud, arrogant, often spoiling for a quarrel, which is the surest means of exercising power. She has reckoned without the signora.

Mrs Proudie cannot be crossed. When the bishop seeks her out in her boudoir to fire the first shots in the Quiverful campaign, she stands her ground and refuses to move. There is no vestige of Christian charity in her uncompromising and blunt stance: 'If Mr Harding is fool enough to tell his tale, we can also tell ours. The place was offered to him, and he refused it. It has now been given to someone else, and there's an end of it. At least I should think so' (p. 143). Here the language is the woman, with three balancing statements, each given an emphatic assertion which brooks no argument, the three followed by the uncompromising 'I'. She sees through the machinations of Slope, whether they are political or amatory: 'I'll Slope him . . . I believe he thinks he is to be Bishop of Barchester himself' (p. 143). Trollope's comic sense is much in evidence, for this is rich indeed coming from the all-powerful prelatess! She maintains her attack upon Slope, but the latter's infatuation with the signora is too pervasive for him to be moved. In any case, in some ways he wishes for and relishes the battle with his patroness. She fires a parting shot to Slope, which is something of an understatement, saying, 'If his lordship wants advice, he knows where to look for it' (p. 146). The unvoiced words are that there is only one person who will be permitted to give it to him.

In Mrs Proudie's case pride certainly comes before a fall. She refuses to let the bishop spend a few days with the archbishop since he has not been invited as a married man and therefore cannot take the lady-bishop with him. 'Mrs Proudie Wrestles and Gets a Fall' is a significant chapter in the power struggle, since Slope wins this battle but loses the war. The bishop's rebellion initially consists of opening the letter to the archbishop which his wife had seen sealed. In the exchange which follows, Mrs Proudie's voice is described as 'imperious', she is 'an unfuriated dame', and her cross-questioning of Slope is for the moment ineffectual. Her power is threatened, and she sees the situation in terms of 'rebellion': 'Anarchy and misrule would quickly follow, unless she took immediate and strong measures to put down the conspiracy which she had detected' (p. 232).

The bishop as conspirator enjoys his temporary triumph, but Mrs Proudie knows that she will rule. She has a cunning beyond her husband's knowledge. The bishop will now be allowed to go unhindered on his visit, but the Quiverfuls will have the hospital. That is the price he must pay for refusing to put down Slope. Mrs Proudie knows her husband only too well. The thought of being a few days away from the palace, from 'the battle-field', 'the dust and heat of the day' (p. 232) which he has just survived, is sop enough for him. In a superb rhetorical aside Trollope asks (of Slope): 'Can you provide that they (the bishop and Mrs Proudie) shall be separated at bed and board?' (p. 234). The line of rhetorical questions reflects the ultimate hopelessness of Slope's position and the absoluteness of Mrs Proudie's power. At this stage that power is in abeyance. Mrs Proudie successfully channels her defeat into reprimanding Mrs Quiverful on account of her husband's weakness. It is a premeditated assertion of power over one whom she considers as a social inferior, but power also consists in patronage, and Mrs Proudie exercises hers with this beaten-down woman. There is something sadistic in Mrs Proudie's tone, but although Trollope concedes that Mrs Proudie is being represented as a female devil, he also says that she is touched by Mrs Quiverful's plight and that of her fourteen children. This moment of weakness in Mrs Proudie, like weaknesses in Harding and the archdeacon, has the effect of humanizing her.

Mrs Proudie is much absent from the overall action while her now despised protégé continues his self-advancing activities. But when she appears she commands attention because of her acerbity, her aggressive and critical moods, her religiosity and her consciousness of status. The military and sometimes epic (or mock-epic) imagery which attends the warring factions in the diocese is concentric unto Mrs Proudie, with references to 'continual victory', 'standards', 'that militant lady' and 'she might yet hurl Mr Slope down to the dust from which she had plucked him' (p. 293).

Her immediate strategy is clear. She takes her coffee in her bedroom, she is 'indisposed'. The implication is that the bishop is responsible for her indisposition. This is how Mrs Proudie exercises power in the domestic arena, since she knows how her husband will feel and is able to calculate how best to play the cards of her moods. The approaching death of the dean shows that fate is on the side of Mrs Proudie against Slope, for the bishop, as I have said, is rather shocked by his chaplain's impudence in putting himself forward for the position. Mrs Proudie is outraged. Before she is moved to violent anger against Slope's ambition, however, she cleverly cross-questions the bishop about the appointment. This shows how easily, confidently, she has resumed the reins of power. She has noted Slope's manoeuvres, and soon faces her husband with the chaplain's unsuitability.

In an elaborate joke about *The Taming of the Shrew* Trollope demonstrates that Mrs Proudie wears the trousers. 'Dean of Barchester, indeed! I'll dean him,' she says, while her 'foot worked on the hearthrug with great rapidity' and 'Mrs Proudie smiled, as a hyena may probably smile before he begins his laugh' (pp. 314–15), all calculated to let the bishop know that he is in error if he hopes to get rid of his chaplain by having him elevated to the deanery. That way lies hypocrisy, and Mrs Proudie will have none of it. She reverts to her condemnation of his association with the signora, damns the hedonistic Stanhopes in her stride, and ends her fulminations about Slope, saying that the man 'has gone mad with arrogance' (p. 316). Sexual jealousy runs to revenge when she adds that she wants 'Mr Slope to appear just what he is – a false, designing, mean intriguing man' (p. 316). She has come full circle from her fulsome praise of Slope's Barchester sermon ('Bishop, did you ever hear a more sublime, more spirit-moving, more appropriate discourse than that?' p. 73). Such is the psychological control of Trollope that Mrs Proudie is revealed directly through her words. Like her language, her moods are wild and various, and might be interpreted as the manifestations of the menopause.

Mrs Proudie at Ullathorne reveals another side to her character, but one that arises again from her drive to power. U. C. Knoepflmacher has perceptively noted the effect of Ullathorne on other characters:

> It is at Ullathorne that Bertie Stanhope reveals truths he would not have dared to utter in Barchester; at Ullathorne where Eleanor tells her father what she would not openly admit in Dr Grantly's house; at Ullathorne where the stiff Mr Arabin finally manages to say 'Eleanor' instead of 'Mrs Bold'.
>
> (*Laughter and Despair*, p. 28)

We might add that it is at Ullathorne that Mrs Proudie displays one of the salient features of her character in her courting of power. She is a snob, delighting to speak to Lady De Courcy on terms of spurious equality and to join with her in their condemnation of the signora and her wiles. Mrs Proudie stoops to abuse and to indulge in gossip. That brilliant comic interplay which Trollope is adept at deploying is seen here in the manifest pleasure Lady De Courcy takes in hearing Mrs Proudie's story. The prelatess runs the whole gamut of censure, calling Madeline 'an abominable woman' and 'the most insolent creature I ever put my eyes on' (p. 355). She exposes her jealousy further by explaining to the 'delighted' countess that Madeline has ruined Slope. She draws attention to Madeline's treacherous eyes, links Bertie to her as an infidel and, as Trollope neatly puts it, 'was therefore able to enjoy the luxury of hating her, without the drawback of wishing her eventually well out of her sins' (p. 357). The comment is an interesting one, for it shows how deep Mrs Proudie's feelings run and how singularly lacking in Christian charity she is. Mrs Proudie is always ruled by her heart rather than her head, but the gossip with Lady De Courcy, despite Trollope's humorous treatment, is inlaid with malice. Hitherto it would have been possible, at a stretch, to consider that Mrs Proudie was actuated by religious motives, that in supporting Slope she was advocating her own sincere brand of

Low-Church Christianity, hence her objection to Mr Harding and the archdeacon. But such a view is untenable after we have seen her at Ullathorne. Mrs Proudie deteriorates rather than improves. Petty, spiteful, vindictive, she diminishes herself through her words, and she also diminishes her husband.

She orders him to sign the Quiverful appointment ('Oh, husbands, oh, my marital friends, what great comfort is there to be derived from a wife well obeyed!', observes Trollope ironically). Mrs Quiverful applies an appropriate image to describe Mrs Proudie: 'She's stiff and hard and proud as pie-crust, but I think she's right at bottom' (p. 411). *We* don't. When Mrs Proudie meets Dr Gwynne her lack of tact discomforts him. She just will not leave, but then Mrs Proudie *is* the bishop, and only once to our knowledge has she left her husband to be his own man when Church affairs are involved. Such is her sense of power that she is moved to anger when Dr Gwynne makes clear his quiet wish to see the bishop alone, and Dr Gwynne is forced to leave, having received the news of Quiverful's appointment from her lips. She has shown her power, further diminished the bishop in the eyes of his peers, made herself disliked, unpopular, resented. Above all, she has succeeded in making her husband look a fool.

As the opposite faction are preparing their triumph with Mr Harding's idea of getting Arabin into the deanery, Mrs Proudie dismisses Slope. I say 'Mrs Proudie' does this because both he and she know it. He realizes that he has been checkmated since 'the confidential doings of the diocese had passed into other hands' (p. 482). Trollope plays neatly on the words 'gentleman bishop' and 'lady bishop'. The latter inspires in the former a parrot-voiced echo of what she says. '"You hear what Mrs Proudie says," said the bishop' (p. 485), and indeed we all do. Some of what she says is bitterly rooted in her sexual disgust. She asks, 'Do you think I have not heard of your kneeling at that creature's feet – that is, if she has any feet – and of your constant slobbering over her hand?' (p. 485). We suspect that Slope slobbered over Mrs Proudie as his benefactress, but that lady is now bent on revenge. With unchristian finality she says that Slope might, conditional upon good behaviour, become curate to Quiverful at Puddingdale.

Mrs Proudie has rightly been regarded as one of Trollope's greatest characters. She is irascible, irritable beyond endurance, strong, assertive, a positive organizer who is lacking in humility and gracious behaviour. She is forthright and impetuous, subscribing to the ideals and practice of the Low Church without practising Christian charity and forbearance herself. She is a strong woman married to a weak and dull man without the character to oppose her wishes or to resist the directions she forces upon him. Mrs Proudie is the woman, and there must have been many in her day, for whom marriage and the domestic role are not enough. It is not merely a question of her ruling her husband. It is more the realization of a driving ambition which takes her beyond the confines of family life. She has no official capacity, she is too naturally autocratic to have any diplomacy, yet we are aware of her capability and of something more. Without her, it seems unlikely that the bishop would be a bishop. There is evidence too, as I have suggested, of sexual sublimation and at times an hysterical behaviour which could be interpreted as menopausal.

Madeline Neroni

The signora stands – or rather lies – in complete contrast to Mrs Proudie. She raises flirtation to a fine art, tasting in her mastery of the arts of attraction something of the sweetness of power. The retrospective introduction of the Stanhope family makes it clear that Madeline is used to having her own way, that she has no intention of forsaking a dominant role in the world. There is a particular concentration on her eyes; they were 'bright as Lucifer's' and 'There was talent in them, and the fire of passion, and the play of wit, but there was no love. Cruelty was there instead, and courage, a desire of masterhood, cunning, and a wish for mischief. And yet, as eyes, they were very beautiful' (p. 67).

This picture prepares us for Madeline, but it cannot do justice to her magnetism. She is regarded by her *bon viveur* father and her indolent mother as a nuisance, though they pet and indulge her. Madeline is art and artifice personified. Any pity we feel at her deprivation is turned to wonder at the compelling effrontery and the poise which she presents to the world. Men come to her couch and find themselves unable to move from it, so quickly enmeshed are they that they must stay to look and listen. Trollope describes her as a basilisk. In fact she has turned to unique advantage her legacy of suffering. It takes force of character to win and maintain power, and Madeline has extraordinary will-power. We may be morally repelled, but we cannot help admiring. Madeline has conquered the world, but it is at best only a small world. There will be no consummation, no love for her, ever; all has been reduced to a power game, an exercise of personality and sexual attraction with no promises. It is a permanent act which is the substitute for living.

Part of Madeline's success consists in the ability to project herself before she arrives. Thus her determination to 'secure the entire use of a sofa' (p. 77) gives her the advance publicity which she needs in order to exercise what her father calls her 'lures'. That advance publicity produces comic effects with the bishop, for example, all agog at the thought of her having no legs. Madeline's art is extended particularly to entrances – I don't know that she is quite as good at exits – and positioning. Since she is intent on performance – this is her life – she 'sent a servant to learn whether it was a right- or a left-hand sofa' (p. 81). Madeline leaves nothing to chance. In the war imagery of the novel, her campaigns are planned and then strategically executed.

Unlike Mrs Proudie, whose power is dependent on temper and autocracy, the signora's power rests on careful preparation that what there is to be seen of her shall be displayed to the fullest advantage. Unlike the archdeacon, she does not need rhetoric or the anger of conflict in order to assert her power. Madeline merely needs a gathering of males of any age to pay her homage. She talks to Slope and not Mrs Proudie and, as we have seen, she laughs when Bertie inadvertently humiliates the prelatess, and speaks 'playfully' to him when he adopts his ridiculously apologetic postures. It is typical of Madeline that she immediately succeeds in ingratiating herself with the bishop, making sure that he is flattered into believing that she is there on his account only. She 'just touched the corner of her eyes with the most lovely of pocket-handkerchiefs' and 'the bishop's arm with her own hand' (p. 87). All this is prelude to asking the bishop personally to bless her child. He is already 'my friend' to her. The 'lures' work at all levels, and part of the comedy consists in the fact that the bishop does not know who she is.

There are no images which can accurately convey her fascination. The sofa at the reception, at Ullathorne and at the Stanhope home is the centre. She affects not to eat, but eats; she is adept at entering into and subtly dominating any conversation. She even turns the discussion of Sabbath-day schools to her advantage with considerable pathos when she observes that 'as she could not possibly go to the children, she might be indulged in the wish of her heart by having the children brought to her' (p. 93). She gains power through her helplessness and enemies through her laughter, which follows Mrs Proudie down the stairs. She has a wonderful fluency, a rapier wit and an irony which is considerably more effective than the bludgeoning bluntness of Mrs Proudie. Madeline is the mistress of many turns of phrase, but they are all calculated to ensure that she dominates. As I have said, sympathy does not entirely desert her. At the Stanhope home, when she is not so elaborately prepared and dressed for occasion, 'there was a look of care and pain about her eyes' (p. 124). There is 'a sort of harsh sadness in her tone'

(p. 124) and Bertie is duly repentant. We see something of the deep bitterness within Madeline. She is unpleasantly critical of Eleanor ('The signora never allowed any woman to be beautiful' p. 124) and bitterly condemnatory of the trappings of widowhood ('I hate such shallow false pretences' p. 125). Her cynicism is shown when she tells Bertie 'I dare say she's to be had for the asking' (p. 126).

The bitterness is very much in evidence in the domestic debate which occurs when Charlotte decides that one of the ways out of their economic troubles is to have Bertie marry Eleanor. Madeline's words on marriage are radical and unequivocal. They may not reflect Trollope's view – indeed, there is no reason why they should – but they are unusual and somewhat daring for their time: '. . . you know what freedom a man claims for himself, what slavery he would exact from his wife if he could! And you know also how wives generally obey. Marriage means tyranny on one side and deceit on the other' (p. 126).

These words not only indicate Madeline's views on marriage, they show something of her drive for power. Just as the jealous Mrs Proudie wishes to be revenged on Slope, so Madeline wishes to be revenged on Signor Neroni, taking all men as her fodder, by fascinating them, torturing them, discarding them. The revenge motive, so integral a part of the Jacobean tragedies loved by Trollope, is given here a powerful and original twist. Men are not party to Madeline's inner thoughts. She is an actress who can easily assume a comic or a tragic part, and does so at the drop of a handkerchief. If the female spider eats the male after copulation, Madeline, so to speak, eats them before. She is a hypnotic temptress who, as in the case of Slope, despatches men before they can get close enough to threaten her.

Despite the centrality of the power theme it is just possible that Trollope realized with Madeline, as did Thackeray in *Vanity Fair* with Becky Sharp, that by concentrating the narrative too heavily on Madeline, he was in danger of doing a disservice to his real heroine, Eleanor. He redresses the balance in a figurative sentence which is uncharacteristically bathetic: 'A sudden half-hour with the Neroni, was like falling into a pit; an evening spent with Eleanor like an unexpected ramble in some quiet fields of asphodel' (p. 129). Eleanor is brought closer to the foreground of the action with her visit to the Stanhopes. During the visit Madeline, knowing of Charlotte's plans for Bertie, agrees to be left alone while the party goes outside. She is an accomplished performer and knows how to command attention, alternating from her sad and lonely reading to uttering whispers which 'could only be heard by the ear into which they were poured' (p. 163), in this instance that of

Mr Slope. She has kept her eyes on Eleanor and come to her own conclusions, and she is later to put her study to good effect.

Slope continues to pursue Madeline, though aware that 'she was a helpless, hopeless cripple' (p. 241). The signora's consciousness of her power over him is conveyed by Trollope in appropriate imagery, describing Slope as 'the finest fly that Barchester had hitherto afforded to her web . . . the signora was a powerful spider, that made wondrous webs, and could in no way live without catching flies' (p. 242). In conveying her need to exercise her power – 'now nearly the only food for her ambition' (p. 242) – Trollope proceeds to the torture image which defines the quality of Madeline's sadism: 'The signora spotted him [Slope], as a boy does a cockchafer on a cork, that she might enjoy the energetic agony of his gyrations' (p. 242).

Trollope, with his mock-heroic irony, compares her to Venus, and Madeline herself finds analogies with Dido and Cleopatra. She demolishes the notion of love by citing literary and pagan references to doomed passion to support her case, such as Juliet, Haidee (Don Juan), Dido, Cressida, Desdemona and Ophelia. We can detect Trollope's characteristic humour when she observes that there is 'no happiness in love, except at the end of an English novel' (p. 245), and when Slope says that her love would 'be sufficient to satisfy the dream of a monarch', she counters with the incisive: 'Say an archbishop, Mr Slope' (p. 247). She outwits Slope at every turn, forcing him to confess his 'love' for her, and then teasing and taxing him about Eleanor. After he has 'caught her hand and devoured it with kisses' (p. 249) she even has the audacity to introduce the name of Signor Neroni into the conversation. Now thoroughly enjoying her capacity to torment him to the highest pitch, she tells him that she is free and invites him to take her, to 'sacrifice the world, and prove yourself a true man' (p. 251). Bluff is the name of the signora's game, but there is a hint of self-pity when she tells him that he has 'fat rectories to get, and possible bishoprics to enjoy . . . you would not sacrifice such things for the smiles of a lame lady?' (p. 252). In Madeline we see a highly sophisticated intriguer whose power, which she relishes to an almost sadistic degree, masks her bitterness.

Madeline's arrival at Ullathorne is as impressive as her entrance at Mrs Proudie's reception. She ingratiates herself immediately with Miss Thorne – Madeline rehearses everything – but suffers a temporary social eclipse with the arrival of Lady De Courcy. Madeline provides immediate fuel for gossip (and enjoys doing so), but not before she has put down Lady De Courcy in an eyeball to eyeball confrontation which leaves that lady no alternative but to make her way on to the lawn. Madeline makes sure that Lady De Courcy hears her say, 'Who on earth is that woman, Mr Slope?' (p. 353). As Trollope puts it, the inherited power of thirty centuries cannot compete with Madeline, whose sensual and intellectual prowess is too much for most women and all men. The signora doesn't hear herself abused but she knows all about it. She is intent on capturing Mr Thorne, even to the extent of inveigling him into seeing 'the last of the Neros' (p. 357). That susceptible man is replaced at the signora's side by the equally susceptible Mr Arabin. From her position Eleanor can see him 'hanging enraptured and alone over the signora's sofa' (p. 360). It is an important moment, for doubtless Eleanor comes to a greater awareness of Mr Arabin's worth at that moment when his seduction seems probable, while the signora, who has some sensibility as well, sees into the exceptional qualities of Arabin and perhaps, too, his suitability for Eleanor. Madeline does more than that. She sees that they are in love, and later transcends her own frustrated existence by bringing them together and promoting their happiness.

This development in character, which seems to be an unpredictable, even unconvincing, move, is, in fact, anticipated in commentary when Trollope observes that she 'had a sort of instinctive knowledge that Mr Arabin was an admirer of Mrs Bold' (p. 363). The way Madeline sets about bringing them together requires, in the first instance, the exercise of her power. It is Arabin's unusually intellectual and gentlemanly qualities which make her rise to the challenge. She is intuitive enough to see that he requires charming, that he is miserable, that he is jealous of Slope, and that he needs her to show him that this is the case. This suits Madeline as she always craves new sensations. She loves to gamble in conversation and with emotions, and 'was rather in hopes that she would ultimately succeed in inducing Mr Arabin to abuse her' (p. 367). This doesn't happen, but she goes to the extremes of audacity in drawing Mr Arabin's attention to Eleanor and asking 'What would you say to her as a companion for life?' (p. 367).

Madeline, however, will not suffer Arabin to dwell too long on Eleanor's virtues. She sends Arabin to get her food because she does not intend to hear (she interrupts him four times to prevent him uttering it) his praise of Eleanor. She does not wish to hear that he considers Eleanor superior to herself. Madeline is adept at extempore wit and raillery – 'I will not hear a word about Mrs Bold. Dread thoughts of strychnine did pass across my brain, but she is welcome to the second place' (p. 368). She ponders the extent of the power she has exerted over Arabin until she no longer knows whether to like him or despise him for his 'facile openness', but considers 'whether she could not do him a good turn'

(p. 371). Even her decision is characterized by her wish for power. That decision is important to the plot and gives Madeline a clear moral direction in that she senses that Bertie will fail with Eleanor and determines to 'give up Mr Arabin to the woman whom he loved' (p. 371).

Her manner of so doing is characteristically forthright. Her letter inviting Eleanor to call upon her is masterly in its directness, economy and reassurance, for Madeline is the mistress of mood and matter. This she demonstrates in her handling of Eleanor, in the bluntness of the signora's language, her speaking of love where Eleanor would have chosen reticence, her advocacy of Arabin because of his qualities as a man, coupled with the brave, wistful longing: 'What would I not give to be loved in such a way by such a man, that is, if I were an object fit for any man to love!' (p. 439). Eleanor is so moved, both by compassion and, almost certainly by the revelation Madeline imparted, that she puts her hand 'caressingly' on Madeline's. The latter tells her with exquisite consideration to leave because she is 'fluttered' but, returning to her more peremptory manner, she tells Eleanor that when she has become happy with Arabin 'I shall expect you to write me one line to say that you have forgiven the sins of the family' (p. 440). Madeline has once more displayed her power in showing how she can influence people and events, but here it is in the interests of the human heart she affects to despise. It is a further rounding of her character.

Her follow-up to this good action is to reduce, humiliate and banish Slope. First she fascinates Arabin with her 'invincible' eyes, and then, already annoyed by Slope's laughter at his failure with the last of the Neros, plays off Slope against his ageing competitor Mr Thorne. Madeline now plays her favourite, provocative power game. She twits Slope over his proposal to Eleanor in front of Arabin. It is as if the sadist, in reaction to that passing kindness to Eleanor, is now intent on drawing blood from Slope who is 'red as a carbuncle and mute as a fish' (p. 447). She is merciless and determined to put Slope down 'now that she had him in her power' (p. 447). There follows the adaptation of 'It's gude to be merry and wise', with 'Mr Slope' tacked on in lines one and three (a device which anticipates Silas Wegg's practice with Mr Boffin in Charles Dickens's *Our Mutual Friend*). Madeline is tired of Slope and gets rid of him with her degrading and demonic laughter.

Our response to Madeline is conditioned by the alternating lightness and darkness of Trollope's controlling touch. Bitter but not bowed, deformed but not degraded, Madeline Neroni is a vivid and colourful character. Her arrogation of power and her employment of it is rooted in her magnetic sensual attraction, her eyes speaking and promising more than her hidden limbs can. She is capable of the most startling fluency, commanding a range from blunt directness to sophisticated innuendo. Part of her power lies in her intellect, which has all the qualities necessary for cynical or playful manipulation. Deprived, she rules, but we never forget the deprivation. Back in Como, she gets the letter she has asked for from Eleanor.

The Archdeacon

The theme of power and its corruptive influence can be seen in another light in the character of the archdeacon. He is initially the victim of chance, for he finds himself rejected as bishop because of a change of ministry. Trollope's account of the archdeacon and his thoughts on gaining the bishopric is masterly. The commentary as he sits watching his dying father and contemplating his own ambitions, humanizes the archdeacon, who is to fall foul of the reader's sympathies on a number of occasions during the narrative. He asks himself 'whether he really longed for his father's death': 'The effort was a salutary one, and the question was answered in a moment. The proud, wishful, worldly man sank on his knees by the bedside, and taking the bishop's hand within his own, prayed eagerly that his sins might be forgiven him' (p. 3). It is a moment of rare humility in the archdeacon, who nevertheless recovers quickly enough from this thought and his father's death. The practicalities of power are peremptory, and he amazes his father-in-law by the speed with which he has the telegram despatched. The irony, as critics have pointed out, lies in the fact that Harding already knows – though he only reveals this as he is about to take the telegram – that the old ministry has fallen.

Although we have seen the archdeacon angry and frustrated in *The Warden*, here he appears softened by the situation. His morning call to greet the new bishop at the palace changes all that. We are told that previously he 'had maintained his power without becoming unpopular' and that 'it may be presumed that he had exercised some wisdom' (p. 27). There was little evidence of that wisdom in *The Warden*, and certainly his subsequent behaviour is open to question. A gentleman with refined tastes, enjoying good living and the benevolent exercise of authority with his local clergy and in his own home (though his wife Susan has much power behind the bed-curtain), Dr Grantly is proud and cannot bear to be crossed. Small wonder that faced with the subversive Proudie and Slope team he reacts with steaming forehead, a sequence of 'Good Heavens!' and scarcely restrained anger. Under his father the archdeacon had been allowed to do much as he wished, and this makes the impact of the vulgarian Slope and the prelatess all the more intolerable to him. Rich himself, he is inclined to think more of the dividends of the railway company rather than the 'offence' of sabbath-day travel. He endures the account of the 'palatial dilapidations' but interrupts them loudly to inform them that any complaints should be addressed to the 'diocesan architect'.

His 'noble wrath' when they leave is accorded the Trollopian mock-heroic style, and an appropriate image comparing him to a steam engine. The wrath soon ceases to be noble and becomes inflammatory as he condemns Slope and Mrs Proudie. In truth his comfortable, rather complacent power has been undermined, and he resolves on war. He impersonates Slope, associating him with a 'set of canting, low-bred hypocrites who are wriggling their way in among us' (p. 39). Now the archdeacon represents the High Church in reaction against this disagreeable manifestation of the Low Church, but he has never been extreme. With war imminent, the only way to assert his power is to rest on the forms and ceremonies, 'the full power of convocation and the renewal of all its ancient privileges' (p. 40). It is typical of Grantly to respond in this way; he is impetuous in judgement and action, and 'was going to fight because he found that he hated the man' (p. 41).

Slope's sermon in the cathedral indicates his own preparations for war, but in the reaction to it (in the chapter entitled 'The Dean and Chapter Take Counsel') it is the archdeacon's voice which is predictably the most powerful. He says that in future Slope must be excluded from the cathedral pulpit. He gets his own way, for they were 'too long accustomed to his rule to shake it off so soon' (p. 52). The archdeacon, intent on observing the correct forms and to be seen to be paying respect to the bishop, goes to Mrs Proudie's reception. This gives him a chance to gain a potential ally by cultivating the returning Dr Stanhope. He has, of course, a closer ally at his side, since Mrs Grantly feels that Slope and 'his assumed dominion in the diocese was a spiritual injury to her husband' (p. 108). She becomes the vigorous 'general of the Grantlyite forces' (p. 108). Her alliance with her husband is an important plot emphasis, since they are both going to become strongly – and misguidedly – concerned that Eleanor is showing all the signs of being about to marry Slope. Meanwhile the archdeacon conducts his own campaign, which is aimed at the defeat of Slope (and, by inference, of Mrs Proudie) by persuading Mr Arabin, the High-Church polemical antagonist of Slope, to accept the living of St Ewold's. This is a political move; it is functional to the plot, but also has the irony that the archdeacon is unknowingly providing Slope with an antagonist in love. Soon the archdeacon has to combat his father-in-law over the terms of the latter's resuming the wardenship, and with typical energy and courage (which he never lacks) Grantly suggests that he himself should see the bishop. Before that he hears from his wife that Eleanor seems to be encouraging the attentions of Slope. With this in mind, and fearing that Slope will buy off Harding's claim to the wardenship by marrying his daughter, he determines to invite Eleanor to Plumstead in order to get her out of Slope's immediate way. This is tactically sound but emotionally dangerous, for Dr Grantly is unable to let well alone. The propinquity of Eleanor is bound to lead to friction for Dr Grantly has, like her, a quality of impetuosity.

To use his authority in order to influence others is part of the archdeacon's nature, and he employs it here to transform St Ewold's parsonage into a comfortably commodious dwelling, in the Grantly style, for Mr Arabin. He speaks 'in his usual loud clear voice, and with that tone of dictation which was so common to him' (p. 187). He opposes dogmatically the idea of a round table. But soon he has to deal with things which appear to be of greater moment, for Slope's letter to Eleanor is put into his hands at Plumstead. The war is being carried into his family. He immediately brings pressure to bear on his father-in-law and erroneously concludes that Eleanor will now marry Slope. The archdeacon's limitations are described thus by Trollope:

> His feelings towards his friends were, that while they stuck to him he would stick to them; that he would work with them shoulder to shoulder; that he would be faithful to the faithful. He knew nothing of that beautiful love which can be true to a false friend. (p. 257)

This goes some way to explain the arrogance and anger of the archdeacon when he is crossed. In a sense he considers Eleanor a disloyal member of the family (he even remembers that he did not like John Bold), and his manner to Eleanor on the slight evidence of Slope's letter is inexcusable. He commissions Mrs Grantly to speak to her, unwise though this is, and then compounds the misguidedness of his stance by saying that he will speak to Eleanor himself. All this should compel our sympathy for Eleanor, and up to a point it does. But the archdeacon's own uncertainty is conveyed to us by a close look at his reactions which follow the arrogance and impetuosity typical of his behaviour. He feels that 'he was sinning against hospitality in upbraiding Eleanor in his own house' and 'he was not quite sure that he would get the best of it' (p. 267). These feelings indicate the depth Trollope brings to bear in his study of this powerful man confronting adversity. What he lacks in humility, however, he makes up for in his sense of duty. This is paramount, and will not let him rest until he has spoken to Eleanor.

When he does so he uses strong words, such as 'suspicion', which show that he has learned little diplomacy, but he meets with 'an amount of compliance which he had not at all expected' (p. 269) when Eleanor puts Slope's letter into his hands. If he needed any convincing that Slope is Eleanor's admitted lover, he needs no more now. His conclusions lead him to giving her an ultimatum which demonstrates not only his mistreatment of Eleanor but also an inbred snobbery and arrogance. He puts it thus: 'You must choose between your sister and myself and our friends, and Mr Slope and his friends . . . I have known the world longer than you have done. Mr Slope is altogether beneath you' (p. 271).

The archdeacon then makes an even worse error by admitting that he has consulted Mr Arabin, 'who agrees with me and Susan that it is quite impossible you should be received at Plumstead as Mrs Slope' (p. 271). He fails to notice Eleanor's confusion at this point which shows, I suggest, that for all the archdeacon's knowledge of the world he has acquired but little knowledge of the human heart. Eleanor, in disgust, rightly calls him 'impertinent'. Trollope indicates that the archdeacon has mishandled the situation because he has made no effort to understand it, that he regards 'her supposed union with disgust: but it never occurred to him that Eleanor was outraged, because she looked at it exactly in the same light' (pp. 272–3). Moreover Grantly has risked his wife's opposition, since she is unlikely to agree to turn Eleanor out of the house.

How is it that Trollope is successful in making the archdeacon the recipient of our sympathy, even our affection, despite the worldly concern with power to which he is so willingly subject? The answer lies, I think, in what has been called the evenness, the levelness, of Trollope's style. The archdeacon's human failings are not given an unconsidered stress, but are integrated into a balanced and careful portrait of the man.

The archdeacon, unlike Mrs Proudie, Slope or Madeline, can be restrained from over-exerting his often misguided authority by the cooler mind and persuasive powers of his wife. I do not intend here to give any in-depth study of Susan Grantly – indeed Trollope does not give us one – except to say this: just as the archdeacon's attitudes are determined by his public position of authority, so Susan Grantly is conditioned by her domestic role. She wields power in the domestic arena just as the archdeacon does in public life. But in their marriage there is little doubt that she is the more powerful of the two. Though occasionally in error, she is less subject to the vagaries of mood. She is able to keep under control the archdeacon's initial irrational impulses, but she is often too late to forestall his misdirections. Although the archdeacon can tell Eleanor that his views are not prejudiced, Susan Grantly knows him well enough to evaluate his wrong-headedness. It is her influence within the matrimonial scene which tempers his public and private explosions. And this she achieves without any undermining of his authority.

The archdeacon is rarely at a loss for words, but he is almost reduced to frustrated silence when it is rumoured that Slope is to be the new dean of Barchester. His world appears to be in danger of being overturned, with war pending in the shape of Eleanor on the domestic front and Slope and the Proudies on the ecclesiastical. Again Trollope's irony plays over these intrigues, for Slope's behaviour has by now alienated Mrs Proudie, making her an unwitting ally of Dr Grantly's. She, too, is unable to countenance 'making such a creature as that [Slope] Dean of Barchester' (p. 315). The archdeacon feels that his life-long area of influence is to be undermined, that 'he should be unable to draw his breath in Barchester Close' if Slope is appointed (p. 319). He jumps to the wrong conclusions here as elsewhere, and much of the dénouement consists of a richly comic sequence which involves successive revelations to the archdeacon – the fact that Eleanor is not going to marry Slope (he was wrong), that she is going to marry Arabin (he was blind), that his father-in-law is going to be offered the deanery ('Good heavens!' he exclaims again). Faced with his will being crossed again in the last instance, since Harding wishes to decline the offer, he becomes very angry and once more tries to exert his power. He succeeds in persuading Harding to reply to the letter and to think things over.

The archdeacon is not simply an autocratic power-seeker. He is warmly responsive, particularly when things turn out to be going his way. The announcement of Eleanor's engagement provokes the three comical exclamations – 'Good heavens!' – and we see some humility in the way he admits that he has been wrong. The engagement of Arabin and Eleanor – how fortuitously things have turned out – finds him acknowledging how 'sly this pair of young turtle doves had been with him. How egregiously they had hoaxed him' (p. 476). He now demonstrates his resilience, falls in with Harding's plan to get the deanery for Arabin, and is graciously approving of Quiverful's having the wardenship. His power is no longer threatened, in fact it has been strengthened by events. He enjoys the joke of telling Arabin that he knows about his engagement, and conducts the marriage service for the happy couple.

We are told that 'the most remarkable feature in the whole occasion was the excessive liberality of the archdeacon. He literally made presents to everybody' (p. 495). This is 'his song of triumph over Mr Slope' (p. 496). The psychological reasons for the gifts are obvious: the archdeacon's power is his security. Where he has been used to rule, to be looked up to, perhaps even to be a little feared, he rules still. Though his 'ecclesiastical authority has been greatly shorn since the palmy days in which he reigned supreme as mayor of the palace to his father' (p. 497) he still enjoys the kind of power which gives him eminence in Barchester. He is a much more vulnerable character than either Slope or Mrs Proudie since he is made to recognize his errors and to find his own ways of acknowledging them. There are times when he appears to have been born for power, and when he wishes to take complete control in trying to ensure that all's right in the Barchester heaven. All too often he is demonstrably wrong, but the compassionate irony which adheres to his presentation makes him a sympathetic and recognizably human character.

The Stanhopes

It is in his portrait of the Stanhopes that Trollope explores the theme of irresponsibility, giving us a picture of the family that is both dark and light in tone. Trollope's satire here is directed towards the absentee churchmen who caused so much anger at this period.

The Stanhopes have spent twelve years on the shores of Lake Como before they are summoned back to England. The signora has had a degrading and mutilating love affair; Bertie has experimented with a number of life-styles, both spiritual and practical, which have come to nothing; Dr Stanhope, who lives for his food, has watched the years pass without any thought of his duties; and Mrs Stanhope, regarding 'a state of inactivity as the only earthly good' (p. 63), has led a completely indolent existence with no purpose in life but to dress well.

Charlotte Stanhope

Charlotte Stanhope occupies a unique position within the structures of power that we have seen to exist between characters. She is both a dedicated daughter and sister, as well as a manipulator and opportunist, reflecting one aspect of what Trollope describes as the 'heartlessness' of the Stanhopes. At thirty-five Charlotte has achieved the distinction of preventing 'the whole family from falling into utter disrepute and beggary' (p. 64), but she can also claim for herself the dubious honour of confirming her family in their indolent ways and thus ensuring they remain, in every way, as they were.

An interesting comparison can be drawn between Charlotte Stanhope and Amy Dorrit of Charles Dickens's *Little Dorrit* (which was issued in monthly numbers in 1855–7): while Amy is intent on making careers for her brother and sister and deplores the latter's marriage made for financial and social gain, Charlotte is bent on economic survival at all costs and on an advantageous marriage for Bertie.

Bertie Stanhope

Bertie Stanhope is thoroughly irresponsible. He has tried the Bar, then set up to be a painter. Attracted to Catholicism, he is converted by the Jews. He is a sculptor in a meaningless, dilettante kind of way. He is handsome, with striking blue eyes and a patriarchal beard. Although he 'was habitually addicted to making love to ladies, and did so without any scruples of conscience', he also has good nature and conscience enough not 'to pay attention to a girl, if he thought any man was present whom it might suit her to marry' (p. 71). But equally he has no principle and no self-respect. Still dependent on his family to support him, he is described as a drone. In all fairness Bertie's irresponsibility is relieved by the humour of his presentation and by his own casual flouting of convention. He makes a striking impression at Mrs Proudie's reception, being 'dressed in light blue from head to foot' (p. 82). His first words, 'Bishop of Barchester, I presume' (p. 82), show that he has no time for formality or any sense of the deference due to status. The humour derives, in part, from the fact that the bishop doesn't know who he is. Bertie, in easy conversational flow, admits that 'I once had thoughts of being a bishop myself' though he adds, 'But, on the whole, I like the Church of Rome best' (p. 83). Bertie also initiates farce, since his activities are not confined to conversation. He pushes the leg of the sofa into Mrs Proudie's lace train, and then, adding to the scandal, exclaims, 'I'll fly into the looms of the fairies to repair the damage, if you'll only forgive me' (p. 85). Since he is on his knees when he says this, the effect is ludicrous, with Mrs Proudie incensed that she has been made to look ridiculous. When the explosion is over, Bertie, with the invention which is always at his finger tips, blames the fat rector, saying, 'But perhaps you are waiting for preferment, and so I bore it' (p. 86). His finest moments in this sequence are still to come, such as when he observes, 'In Germany, the professors do teach; at Oxford, I believe, they only profess to do so, and sometimes not even that' (p. 90). Variety is the spice of Bertie's life, and before Dr Proudie can escape he tells him 'I was a Jew once myself', thus hastening the bishop's departure.

Bertie is a bubble of irresponsible fun but, like Madeline, faced with the obvious moral decency of Eleanor, he behaves in much the same way as Madeline behaves over Arabin. And just as it is not really self-sacrifice for either of them – for Bertie does not really want the rope of responsibility and marriage – it demonstrates that the young Stanhopes are not heartless. Bertie informing Eleanor of the plan to marry her is balanced by Madeline telling Eleanor in no uncertain terms to marry Arabin: in fact there is a curious family consistency in their actions. It is as if a residue of moral responsibility is present in each of them. Although Trollope refers to Bertie as 'impudent or else mischievous' (p. 95) it would be just as accurate to call him 'engaging and resilient'. He occupies the middle ground somewhere between Slope and Arabin. In his response to 'Lotte' urging him to marry Eleanor he lists Eleanor's advantages with admirable economy and factual verve: 'She's a widow with lots of tin, a fine baby, a beautiful complexion, and the George and Dragon hotel up in the High Street. By Jove, Lotte, if I marry her I'll keep the public house myself – it's just the life to suit me' (p. 124). And it is – until the next enchantment. Without roots, without moral perspective, Bertie is fated to find himself in many a blind alley of enthusiasm.

But Trollope, in a burst of authorial confidence, tells his readers that it 'is not destined that Eleanor shall marry Mr Slope or Bertie Stanhope' (p. 126). Such is our interest in Bertie that this does not seem to matter: we still wait to see how he will conduct himself towards Eleanor. It says much for Trollope's powers of characterization that Bertie moves from a kind of pre-Wodehouse caricature of a young man into a much fuller character, but basically he does not *change*. He merely adopts a low-key approach out of a mixture of decency and self-interest in a highly credible combination. Essentially he is not only resilient but also shallow or, as Trollope puts it, he was 'incapable of anticipating tomorrow's griefs' (p. 155). His father is constantly beset by Bertie's debts, and this provides the motivation, from Charlotte's standpoint, for Bertie to marry Eleanor. He is tactful and shows some sensitivity, but the major trait in his character is self-interest. Barchester and Eleanor by moonlight find him 'amusing and familiar, yet respectful' (p. 164).

Bertie's banter only modulates into seriousness when he decides to reveal the plan to Eleanor. At the back of this scene is Charlotte's knowledge of Bertie's hopeless position with his creditors, and this accounts for her insistence that Bertie should propose to Eleanor, although Charlotte knows that Eleanor has just received a proposal from Slope. Bertie, to do him some credit, does not share his sister's insensitivity. Charlotte arranges the opportunity for him, and Eleanor 'was to be left under Bertie's special protection' (p. 393). His response to the imminence of this situation is given in commentary, heavily alliterative, perhaps to indicate the uncharacteristically strong nature of Bertie's feelings: 'There was a cold, calculating, cautious cunning about this quite at variance with Bertie's character' (p. 401). We might add that the prospect of stagnating in Barchester is not attractive to him either.

He must get out of it somehow, and he decides to do so by the blunt expedient of confiding in Eleanor. The scene is subtly presented, and almost undermines our earlier conception of Bertie's irresponsibility. Eleanor's genuine worth, the sincerity of her interest in him, nearly makes him change his mind about not proposing to her. He jokes his way out of it by picturing to Eleanor his future life-style in Barchester. He determines to base that future on her decision or advice. In a deftly ironic contrivance Trollope has manoeuvred his characters to the exact spot where Eleanor slapped Slope's face. This contributes to the humour of the situation, but Bertie's directness (he can't help telling Eleanor that the whole thing is Charlotte's idea) in saying, 'She wants me to marry you' (p. 406) upsets Eleanor. He is rebuffed by Eleanor, but responds good-naturedly, though he is genuinely moved by Eleanor's tears.

Still he cannot leave things as they are, for his own interests are very much at stake. He asks Eleanor to take part in deceiving Charlotte by saying that Eleanor has turned him down. He obviously fears his sister's (and father's) wrath by this attempt to insure himself against their reactions. Although Eleanor is by now really angry, she allows herself to be mollified by his evident concern for her. She had 'already half-forgiven him before he was at the drawing-room window' (p. 409). Bertie has to ensure his father's justified acerbity of temper and his response is to amuse himself by drawing little pictures of, among others, Mrs Proudie. On the following day he departs for 'the marble quarries of Carrara' (p. 437). Earlier he had made a facetious remark about 'not attempting anything large . . . unless I do my own tombstone' (p. 437). But Bertie is a survivor, and there is little doubt that he and his family, as irresponsible and parasitic as ever, will continue their indolent life-style.

Eleanor Bold

The signora is obviously destined to prey on susceptible males, but the central love theme offers a distinct contrast to her activities. It takes place, of course, between Eleanor and Arabin, whom some critics have seen as dull and uninteresting characters. The consistency of family traits maintained by Trollope in his presentation of character is seen in

Eleanor. She has her sister's pride (and occasional aggression) and her father's obstinacy, her sister's power to influence and her father's sensitivity, though in Eleanor's case this sensitivity is sometimes masked by pride. And just as her father establishes for himself a kind of independence – when he is allowed it by the archdeacon – so Eleanor is demonstrative in her independence, though youthful and spirited in her opposition to the archdeacon. Where Eleanor differs from her father and her sister is in her impetuosity, which makes her turn on the archdeacon and slap Slope. But Eleanor has certain pliant characteristics, and it is because of these that she is unable to gain the upper hand over the signora. Madeline confronts her at a vulnerable time for Eleanor, in the post-Slope pre-Arabin sequence. Eleanor, for all her apparent independence, has a streak of innocence and manifestly cannot cope with Madeline.

Eleanor has had independence thrust upon her in the shape of widowhood. We are told in Trollope's retrospective summary that she had clung to John Bold 'with the perfect tenacity of ivy' (p. 13). But Eleanor is too volatile to spend half a lifetime in grief and loyalty to a memory. She has been left comfortably off by her husband, the ivy loosens its grip, and 'Eleanor's bosom became tranquil' (p. 15). She becomes an object of attraction to Slope when he hears of her inheritance – which might oil the wheels of preferment or cushion non-preferment – and allows herself to be influenced by his ingratiating sympathy and interest. He is, in her somewhat obdurate estimate, 'not quite so black as he had been painted' (p. 55).

Throughout the action of *Barchester Towers* Eleanor's main concern is for her father, at least until she becomes aware of her feelings for Arabin, though there are times when her baby is everything to her. There are moments when she feels that she has been ill-used or when she is bewildered by the state of her emotions. The dullness which critics have seen in Eleanor takes no account of her sense of humour. Learning of the new plans for the hospital she tells her father, 'I won't have a matron for a new stepmother' (p. 57). Naïvely thinking, however, that Slope respects her father, she places herself obstinately on the chaplain's side without initially realizing how others, and more particularly her own family circle, may construe it.

After her father has seen Slope she reveals that she had seen the chaplain the previous day, a tactless revelation in view of her father's misery. Eleanor's innocence in this regard (she is misguided not wilful) is interpreted as evidence of her attachment to Slope by her sister Susan, who tells Mr Harding that 'it was to be expected that Eleanor should marry again' (p. 109).

Eleanor now becomes the subject of speculation and in her reactions to this are displayed much of the obstinacy and independence we see in her. The narrator observes, after the archdeacon's fulminations on the supposed affair, that 'the widow Bold was scandalously ill-treated by her relatives' (p. 117). We must note that Eleanor goes some way towards provoking this treatment. It is not just that she has been susceptible to Slope's oiliness, it is also that she has a commendable sympathy for the underdog, for in High-Church Barchester that is what Slope is. Though Madeline can be contemptuous of Eleanor's observance of her widowhood – 'She is just one of those English nonentities who would tie her head up in a bag for three months every summer, if her mother and her grandmother had tied up their heads before her' (p. 125) – she does her a disservice, for Eleanor is an emotional and vulnerable woman. Trollope presents her with a mixture of romance, sentiment and irony, remarking on her loveliness and the 'character about her mouth' (p. 129) as well as showing her as cloyingly maternal, particularly in the chapter 'Baby Worship'.

Moved deeply by her father's position over the hospital, Eleanor secretly cannot make up her mind whether Slope is 'true or false' (p. 139). She falls foul of the archdeacon by suggesting that he should have seen Slope, and his response makes her feel that 'she was charged with improper conduct' (p. 149). This makes her angry and she leaves with due dignity, though she agrees to go to Plumstead at his request, not knowing that he is cunningly intent on getting her out of Slope's immediate orbit. Though she knows that her father has been softening the archdeacon, she is unaware that the Stanhopes have invited Slope, as well as her, for that evening. Not that it bothers her, for Eleanor has a kind of naïveté and does not suspect at this stage that Slope is interested in her. This ingenuous innocence is to lead to conflict, and there is already the unspoken rivalry between Bertie and Slope. Deliberately left alone with Eleanor, Bertie is given the opportunity to make his suit to her, but does not take advantage of it. She feels, instead, that 'he was one of the most agreeable of men' (p. 164). Eleanor at Plumstead is forced into the position of taking Slope's part, in reaction to her sister, who spends some time in abusing him. Eleanor is perceptive, but she can also be obtuse. For example, she feels that 'Mr Slope found other attraction at Dr Stanhope's' (p. 180). Assuredly he did, but Eleanor is obstinately putting to the back of her mind his own very obvious interest in her.

Arabin is attracted to Eleanor, albeit without knowing it to begin with. When they come together at St Ewold's we can see the schematic pattern Trollope is using to anticipate later events. The focus of the conversation is Arabin's future. Eleanor innocently refers to the priestess of the St Ewold's legend, jokingly remarking that Arabin would oppose the idea of the priestess bearing 'all the sway herself' and adding, 'such might be too much the case now if a sacred lady were admitted within the parish' (p. 182). For the reader, Eleanor's remarks not only inadvertently anticipate her own future position, but also, with Trollope's characteristic irony, lead us to the palace where the priestess – called by the narrator the prelatess – does hold sway. Mrs Grantly immediately picks up the reference. Their exchange lays the foundations for Eleanor's later feelings, and already she is struck by the engaging earnestness of Arabin, and by his contrast to the clergymen of Barchester, for he 'spoke in a manner very different from that to which she was accustomed' (p. 185). Eleanor's intelligence is engaged (Trollope's women are so much more intelligent than Dickens's) and the potential of her character and personality are seen as she questions Arabin, whose sensitivity over his position, and his previous leanings towards Rome, call forth both spirit and sensitivity in Eleanor. This interchange, with its raillery and its emphasis on condemnation ('It is so easy to condemn; and so pleasant too; for eulogy charms no listeners as detraction does' p. 186) signals their attraction through temporary conflict. It also anticipates Eleanor's future condemnation of Arabin's agreement with the archdeacon over her affairs, and his condemnation in turn of Eleanor's supposed relationship with Slope. Again we are aware of Trollope's sense of structure. At this stage the interaction between Eleanor and Arabin is delightful, and we see how securely their future relationship is based.

The influence of Miss Thorne on Eleanor on the subject of matrimony and of abandoning widowhood, is also important, though she tries Eleanor somewhat by nagging her about her child. The next visit to the Stanhopes, in which Mr Arabin 'moth-like, burnt his wings in the flames of the signora's candle' (p. 211), finds Eleanor observing him critically, despite the pleasant distraction of Bertie Stanhope. Trollope hastens to assure us, with direct omniscient intervention, that Eleanor is not in love with Arabin, but then qualifies the statement by observing, 'How many shades there are between love and indifference' (p. 211). There is an authorial definition of perspective: 'But her devotion to her late husband was fast fading when she could resolve in her mind, over the cradle of his infant, the faults and failings of other aspirants to her favour' (p. 212). Eleanor is refreshingly human; like most of us, she does not know herself.

When Slope's letter to Eleanor is delivered at Plumstead it puts her directly under suspicion and confirms the archdeacon's fears. Yet, because she is innocent, Eleanor is disgusted by Slope's vulgar compliment to her tresses. She believes that Slope has really put himself out for her father and that he has virtually assured his return to the hospital. The letter is fraught with immediate consequences, and when Eleanor enters the drawing-room she knows intuitively that they have all been talking about her. The description of her feelings shows how deeply she is moved: 'She felt that she had been tried and found guilty of something' (p. 259). She cannot eat; her vulnerability is fully exposed. She withdraws into herself as the archdeacon's policy is put into effect.

The conflict first surfaces openly in Susan Grantly's approach to Eleanor. Such is the latter's independent spirit that she is moved to rebuff her, knowing full well that behind her sister is the archdeacon. Eleanor is driven to the extremes of reaction partly through the tactlessness and mismanagement of her relatives. She tells Susan with some truth, 'You all want me to be as illiberal as yourselves' (p. 262). The irony of her position is highlighted in the comment that 'she would not join in the persecution, even though she greatly disliked the man' (p. 263). This reference to Slope again shows her obstinacy. As she awaits her father in silence (having determined to show him the letter), she worries lest Arabin should know of her correspondence with Slope, which is again ironic as Arabin has been told that it is very likely she will marry that undesirable! Eleanor – her lack of judgement clearly indicates her innocence – shows her father the letter. She wishes to be cleared of any imputation, but the letter has the reverse effect. This blindness, this strong need for her father's belief in her now that she is beset, shows Eleanor in error, but infinitely humanized by being so. As the narrator observes, 'yet it was the true feminine delicacy of Eleanor's mind which brought on her this condemnation' (p. 265). Eleanor believes in Slope's honesty, and in her openness she has ignored the fact that the tenor of Slope's letter is not going to be received as innocently either by her father or by the archdeacon. Yet in a sense Eleanor is being misjudged on two counts. The first is the assumption that she is going to marry Slope, and the second is that those closest to her do *not* see that it would be repugnant to her to do so, and that they are insulting her by so suggesting.

Eleanor's spirit is fully shown in the confrontation with the archdeacon. Labouring under the insult of his presuming to advise her, she says of her father with simple and unswerving loyalty, 'While he lives I can never want advice' (p. 268). From then on she proceeds to wrong-foot the archdeacon (she gives him Slope's letter before he asks for it) with aggressive pride. She puts herself in the wrong by calling it (out of obstinacy, as Trollope tells us) 'Quite a proper letter' (p. 269). Eleanor is isolated and we are told that no one, not even Mr Harding, has been kind to her. She is humiliated by the archdeacon's reference to her as the future Mrs Slope. She regards it as an insult, and asks the archdeacon, 'How dare you be so impertinent?' (p. 271). Trollope's handling of situation is excellent here. He sees to the heart, and particularly to the heart of his women characters. Eleanor deduces from the archdeacon's words that the suggestion that she will become Mrs Slope emanates from Arabin. This misconception undermines her wish to stand well in Arabin's eyes. It also shows the feeling (witness her jealousy of Arabin's interest in the signora) she has for him and which she cannot, at this stage, either articulate or understand. A close look at the reactions of Eleanor and the archdeacon after their interview shows the irrational bias and dislike which has been engendered by wilful misunderstanding. Yet such is Trollope's awareness of the sincerity of each in this terrible interaction that their complexity is enhanced. A moment of considered thought, an overcoming of obstinacy and pride, would have put all right.

Eleanor suffers the next day because she is able to acknowledge that, although she has been mistreated, she herself is also in error. She is not helped by Arabin. However, when she upbraids him for calumniating her, she does reveal something of her own feelings: 'I must confess, Mr Arabin, that from you I expected a different sort of usage' (p. 281). Injured and angry, Eleanor leaves the room, but is quickly sought out by Arabin, who has discovered the state of his own heart. The two are in conflict based on misunderstanding. It is typical of Eleanor's intransigence that when Arabin is moved to tell her that 'I have esteemed, do esteem you, as I never yet esteemed any woman' (p. 285) she 'walked beside him determined at least to give him no assistance' (p. 285). This is her outward stance, but her inward reactions as she listens to his periphrases are 'a sort of joy' (p. 286).

Still she persists in her obstinate, injured and somewhat vengeful attitude. She is conscious that she is loved but yet is not acknowledging how she herself might respond to this. Eleanor, so vulnerable in her pride, so well-meaning in her intentions, has been deeply injured by the thoughtlessness of others. She has also been injured by her own obstinacy. There is something rather sad in Trollope's irony which exposes poignantly the difference between the appearance and the truth. She is not yet ready to forgive the blameless man who loves her, again demonstrating a wilful independence. Trollope deftly manages this scene in such a way that, though we may feel sorry for Arabin, who finds himself verbally inadequate in an emotional situation which is so new to him, we also feel some admiration, and pity too, for Eleanor in her wounded pride.

There is little wonder that Eleanor turns increasingly to the Stanhopes, enjoying the company of Bertie, and even blushing on one occasion when she calls him by his Christian name. Again we note the naturalness of Eleanor. Previously unconscious of the improprieties in her behaviour with Mr Slope, she is very much more wary in this other situation which, however, appears to be innocent. At this stage Charlotte's plan is working well, and it is helped by the fact that she and her family are 'peculiarly agreeable to Eleanor after the great dose of clerical arrogance which she had lately been constrained to take' (p. 308). Eleanor has escaped Arabin physically, but she is very much aware of his influence upon her, and 'she also looked forward to forgiving him' (p. 308). There is a touch of pique here, for she is still angry enough to 'bite her lip and stamp her foot as she thought of what he had said and done' (p. 308), but the passionate nature of her temperament begins to emerge more fully.

Just as Eleanor is looking forward to seeing Arabin, Charlotte's manoeuvring conveys her to Ullathorne in the same carriage as Slope. Eleanor is anxious that Arabin will notice this, rather than her 'impertinent' brother-in-law, which is evidence of her partiality for Arabin. However, she has no resources to oppose the plan, and is spotted by Arabin. She has been pondering on whether she has been mistaken in her attitude to Slope and whether Slope is, indeed, intending to court her. She becomes very upset (Eleanor is a volatile character) and determines 'to disabuse at any rate her father's mind' about 'the most odious man I ever met in my life' (pp. 346–7). Her passion leads her to condemn the archdeacon verbally. She shudders 'as she thought of the matrimonial torch which her friends had been so ready to light on her behalf' (p. 348). She sheds many tears, despite the comfort (and relief) of her father. But Trollope cunningly emphasizes her feelings for Arabin, which remain unvoiced and covert, in two rhetorical questions: 'And what had Eleanor meant when she declared that *whatever she did* she would tell her father first? What was she thinking of doing?' (p. 349). In fact when Arabin does propose she responds in the way we knew she would – warmly, movingly, tenderly. Later she tells her father.

Before that Eleanor has much to endure. The narrator, deliberately exaggerating the romantic nature of the novel, refers to her performances at Ullathorne as 'melodrama'. It is a neatly ironic perspective, but to Eleanor Slope's proposal followed by the revelations of Bertie are insults, her humiliation brought about partly by her own obstinacy in the first place, and by the wiles of Charlotte Stanhope in the second. Her reactions to both men show her pride and the passionate nature of the woman Arabin is to win. When she slaps Slope the commentary makes clear the nature of her character: 'She was too keen in the feeling of independence, a feeling dangerous for a young woman, but one in which her position peculiarly tempted her to indulge' (p. 385). In reaction against Slope Eleanor flees to the Stanhopes and almost, metaphorically, leaps into the fire. But Bertie undermines his sister's plans and Eleanor, having swallowed her anger and 'played the last act of that day's melodrama' (p. 410), goes home and makes much of her child, a display of maternal feeling which helps to alleviate her sense of humiliation and frustration. Her possessive devotion here again shows the warmth, the passion of her nature. Trollope explains it in a down-to-earth, almost throw-away fashion when he observes: 'This kind of consolation from the world's deceit is very common. Mothers obtain it from their children and men from their dogs' (p. 424).

When her father learns what has happened over Slope, Eleanor's independent spirit rears itself again, and she says that she will not tell the archdeacon or her sister. Having lavished affection on her child, she continues in this strain by urging her father to come and live with her. Her frustrations are brought to an end by the intervention of the signora. She is softened by Madeline, 'stupefied' by what she has heard and by the knowledge that the signora has read her secret. But at last she can recognize her own love and the love of the undeclared Arabin – 'She could not, would not, did not doubt it' (p. 440).

Eleanor has a source of help in Miss Thorne, and Trollope employs a retrospective narrative to inform the reader of Eleanor's engagement before proceeding to dramatize its actuality. Miss Thorne is Arabin's sympathetic advocate before the scene. Eleanor, who has felt the pressure inside her family over Slope, now finds this pressure outside directing her towards Arabin. Eleanor manifests a certain jealousy of the signora, but by now she has received her instructions from that normally unscrupulous siren. When Arabin sees Eleanor the topic of his conversation at first steers well clear from the subject of love, and afterwards, when he is at last so moved that he speaks her name, Eleanor 'looked slowly, gently, almost piteously up into his face' (p. 466). In a finely brief anticipation of the consummation, the narrator observes 'They were the same – one flesh – one spirit – one life' (p. 466).

Eleanor, who has to be alone first to imbibe the full luxury of it, then tells little Johnny Bold, 'all unmeaning to him' of his new father, before taking him to that father in full generosity of love (pp. 467–8). Eleanor has always expressed her liking for old-fashioned things, and becomes increasingly conservative in her religious observances. She has 'put up a memorial window in the cathedral', while her sister believes that she 'will have an oratory in the deanery before she has done' (p. 497).

There is some considerable subtlety in Eleanor's presentation. The nominal heroine of the novel, she has depths, even contradictions, which make for convincing roundedness. The elaborate schema which Trollope constructs in bringing Arabin and Eleanor together enhances both Eleanor's development as a character and our appreciation of her complexity. Eleanor's independent spirit and warmly impetuous nature are happily subsumed in domesticity. It is the classic ending for the Victorian heroine which Trollope, in his final comments, openly, and somewhat ironically, emphasizes.

Francis Arabin

Dean Arabin, as he comes to be, and Eleanor exchange views on worldliness, among other things. Arabin himself is intellectual, unworldly, sincere, given to raillery at times but unsure of himself when confronting an emotion such as love. In this he is inexperienced; he is also, as he acknowledges at St Ewold's, lonely. Trollope's account of Arabin's character balances Arabin's sober past against the immediate attractions of the present, either at Plumstead Episcopi, or standing – and sitting – at the feet of the signora. That Arabin is a well drawn, sympathetic character there is little doubt, though facile identification would be irrelevant here. We see him in the context of his views, which are given firm historical and ecclesiastical veracity, and we also see him drawn into the area of personal emotions which are new to him but, like Eleanor's, are complex and convincing as they unfold. This is due, in part, to the thoroughness of Trollope's portrait of Arabin's past and to Arabin's evident vulnerability.

Arabin stands in direct contradistinction to Slope. He represents High-Church principles and a kind of searching enlightenment, compared with Slope's Low-Church leanings. Trollope makes his bias clear. Slope is destined by the nature of the narrative to fall, at least morally and spiritually, and Arabin is destined to be successful, despite his lack of sophistication and occasional misjudgement. Although he is 'a great pet in the common rooms at Oxford, an eloquent clergyman, a droll, odd, humorous, energetic conscientious man' (p. 111) Arabin has a genuine humility.

I cannot agree with James Kincaid when he observes that 'In the end

Mr Arabin becomes a kind of Mr Harding-in-training, committed to the old-fashioned and accepting from his father-in-law the deanship' (*The Novels of Anthony Trollope*, p. 112). Arabin is a public man, a debater, polemical and witty, and although he has the kind of integrity which his future father-in-law possesses, Eleanor is not marrying him in her father's image. His humility, his capacity to learn, sets him apart from Slope, whose motivation is the self-interest of preferment, or Mrs Proudie, who would not understand Arabin's stance, in either practical or spiritual matters. We are made aware of Arabin's spiritual battle in the past, and it conditions our sympathies in the present. He is an unlikely hero, but it is part of Trollope's narrative concern to present the real rather than the ideal, and to reinforce that realism by integral commentary on thought, emotion, and action. With Arabin, Trollope contrives a masterly consistency. The man who was tempted by dogma, belief and ritual to follow Newman shows himself susceptible to other kinds of temptation, both those of the signora and, more movingly, the natural temptation of a compatible love. This time he succumbs and begins to live.

After the retrospective of Arabin, Trollope characteristically adopts an ironic tone with regard to him. We are told that he 'is worthy of a new volume' (p. 167). His dedication and humour are stressed as well as his active participation in the Tractarian movement which leads him close to temptation. Trollope indulges in his own brand of mildly anti-academic raillery by pointing out that Arabin did not get a double-first, or even a first, but he put 'firsts and double-firsts out of fashion for the year' (p. 169).

Arabin is appointed professor of poetry at Oxford where he nearly becomes a follower of Newman. Trollope, in an emphatic series of rhetorical repetitions, describes how Arabin was tempted to do so, by his heart, his taste, his flesh and his faith. Most important is the fact that he is saved by a humble rural clergyman (perhaps Mr Crawley of *The Last Chronicle*). On his return to Oxford he becomes an important influence in the ecclesiastical life of his times – 'he became known as a man . . . in opposition to anything that savoured of an evangelical bearing' (p. 172). His character has been strengthened by his resistance to temptation; he is a public figure opposed to reform who serves on many committees, but the inner man still feels the need for the annual retreat. That inner man has uncertainties, even frustrations, despite the reputation which the outer man has achieved. We are told of Arabin that there was 'a continual play of lambent fire about his eyes, which gave promise of either pathos or humour whenever he essayed to speak', and, better still, 'his wit never descended to sarcasm' and 'there was no ill-nature in his repartee' (p. 173). Although popular with women, Arabin was ignorant of the workings of the feminine mind. A significant aspect of the development in his character ('women generally were little more to him than children', p. 173) consists of revealing the education of his feelings. He is used to a rational and controlled existence; he finds that at the age of forty his feelings are not dead (witness the signora) and that he can be deeply moved by them into both conflict and sympathy (witness Eleanor). The archdeacon's opinion of him is worth quoting. He says that his friend is 'the most free from any taint of self-conceit. His fault is that he's too diffident' (p. 174).

In Trollope's moral scheme these are virtues, seen by the contrasting light of Slope's self-conceit and pushing nature. Dr Grantly knows his man and knows that Arabin, the public debater, is rather different from Arabin 'in social intercourse with those whom he did not intimately know' (p. 175). Arabin himself thinks that he is a man of 'little consequence'. At the time we meet him he, like Eleanor, is vulnerable, particularly when exposed to domesticity which he feels lacking in his own life. He is tired of college existence, tired of loneliness, somewhat envious of the Grantlys. Trollope's sense of realism makes him paint Arabin not as a saint to match Slope's sinner, but as a self-questioning and self-doubting man.

Arabin's talents and observances are outward compensation for inward frustrations; he is recognizably, and sufferingly, human. We like Arabin for what he is and feel some pity, too, for what he has made himself – a man deprived of human comforts and love. Like Eleanor, he has that streak of independence which has directed his way. Early on he was ambitious to 'strike out a course showing a marked difference from those with whom he consorted. He was ready to be a partisan as long as he was allowed to have a course of action and of thought unlike that of his party' (p. 177). This somewhat headstrong independence has led to a general malaise in middle age. Our sympathy is engaged, and it never leaves Arabin, despite the way he behaves. For all his cleverness, Arabin is an innocent in the ways of the world.

Arabin's initial response to Eleanor is as guarded as we might expect it to be. He merely enjoys the prospect of staying with 'a very pretty woman' (p. 181). His first exchanges with Eleanor, as we have seen, ironically involve matrimony, since Mrs Grantly is intent on teasing him about the possibilities of his bringing a priestess to St Ewold's. His humour is apparent in his remark about 'no priestly pride has ever exceeded that of sacerdotal females' (p. 182), which contains an innuendo about Mrs Proudie. His debate on 'wars about trifles' (p. 183) with

Eleanor hints at their future compatibility. Arabin reveals something of himself, for he is earnest, and conveys to her his 'aspirations after religious purity' (p. 185). He opens Eleanor's mind to real, positive discussion, not one dogmatic or bereft of ideals, but living and vibrant in the man who is speaking. It is a stress-mark in her education, beginning the process, as yet unconsciously, of drawing her towards a love based on true respect. When Eleanor experiences 'a certain pleasurable excitement' (p. 185), we recognize Arabin's unique qualities, the rare integrity of the man. His sincerity is allied to spiritual enlightenment and a knowledge, from his own experience, of the frailty of human nature.

Arabin is nervous when he makes his debut at St Ewold's, though he has the tact and the discipline not to be long-winded. We notice that later he is attentive to Eleanor, explaining to her 'the difference between a naiad and a dryad' (p. 209). We know, however, that he has come under the spell of the signora. Even here there is something innocent about his response, since his contained world of religious debate can have known nothing like Madeline. The fact that he can be easy (if tactless) in the carriage coming home with Eleanor when he says he has never 'met so much suffering joined to such perfect beauty and so clear a mind' (p. 211) shows that he is commendably guileless. Eleanor finds him pleasant but is not always sure that he is in earnest: she reads him very accurately when she feels that it was 'almost as though he were playing with a child' (p. 213). We remember that Arabin himself thought of women as children, is not practised in female company, and is trying to overcome a natural shyness which cannot easily be dispersed. He moves towards her inwardly, and she moves towards him – before his offence with the archdeacon over Slope – without benefit of articulated feelings. For all the romantic overtone there is subtlety, unconscious attraction in these movements; despite the reticence we are aware of sexual awakening.

Situated as he is at Plumstead and in close relation to the archdeacon, Mr Arabin is made privy to the immediate fears about Eleanor and Slope. He is not aware that his own heart is engaged, though we are told that 'he was surprised, vexed, sorrowful and ill at ease' (p. 260) when Eleanor's name is coupled with the chaplain's. He is totally unprepared for the outburst of anger on Eleanor's part, his own modesty prevents him from appreciating that he has provided her with an agreeable and secure basis at Plumstead.

It is when Arabin's name is mentioned by the archdeacon that Eleanor decides that she must leave her brother-in-law's house. Meanwhile, Arabin, the unwitting cause of all this, having heard that 'she loved someone else . . . began to be very fond of her himself' (p. 275). This insecure man becomes obsessed with the idea that Eleanor is going to marry Slope, while he 'was in love without being aware of it' (p. 277). He is no match for Eleanor's mood and temper when they next meet. He is rather put out when he is told that he 'should practise as well as preach' (p. 279), and profoundly moved when he is accused of calumny. Nevertheless, having been consulted by the archdeacon, he sticks to his word despite Eleanor's impassioned denunciation. His reaction to this is warm, human, sexual – 'He had never seen her so excited, he had never seen her look half so beautiful' (p. 282). It is also silent. When he realizes that Eleanor is not going to marry Slope 'he began to be aware that he was himself in love' (p. 283).

There follows his frustrating declaration as Arabin, versed in the rhetoric of debate, uses the rhetoric of love without actually uttering it. His emotional sincerity is so strong that it renders him incapable of the direct assertion he wishes to make. Eleanor is aware that he 'was striving and striving in vain to tell her that his heart was no longer his own' (p. 286). In his tortured anxiety and awakened passion he gives his final utterance the wrong emphasis when he says 'Answer me this one question. You do not love Mr Slope? you do not intend to be his wife?' (p. 286). It is intrusive, what Eleanor regards in the archdeacon as impertinent. Arabin must wait and suffer, reduced, in Trollope's commentary, to an 'untaught, illiterate, boorish, ignorant man!' (p. 287). The heavy irony tells us that he is none of these, but unskilled in the art, language, manners and knowledge of sophisticated love. There can be no greater tribute to his sincerity.

Just as Arabin struggled spiritually on the edge of Catholicism, so he struggles on the edge of his feelings for Eleanor. His outward diffidence contrasts with the searching integrity of the inner man. He is inclined to judge himself over-harshly: 'It was and ever had been his weakness to look for impure motives for his own conduct' (p. 317). He has particular qualms of conscience over Eleanor's fortune (compare this with Slope's unmitigated delight at the prospect of it). He determines not to think of Eleanor, and then thinks all the more about her.

Such is his waywardness that he also thinks of the signora, who has flattered him, listened to him, and called into action the wiles necessary to captivate this susceptible and 'ignorant man'. But Arabin has depths of resilience. He manages to conquer his 'imaginary sorrows and Wertherian grief' (p. 318) and sparkles in conversation at the archdeacon's table. Despite this overt demonstration he has not conquered himself, yet he is still able to give Harding the good advice not to do anything about the hospital until he hears from the bishop.

After his arrival at Ullathorne Sports he sees Eleanor alight from the Stanhope coach assisted by Mr Slope, but does not hear Eleanor enlighten her father about that 'odious man'. He is not happy as he ponders on Eleanor's behaviour, but he is fair and reasonable enough to consider that she may have defended Slope on principle, and that 'in itself would be admirable, lovable, womanly' (p. 361). He is regarded by the signora as a different species to those she usually hunts, and he is bewildered, as Eleanor is later, by her ability to read the secrets of his heart, and by such outrageous questions as: 'There is the widow Bold looking round at you from her chair this minute. What would you say to her as a companion for life?' (p. 367). It is a rhetorical question. Arabin naturally does not enjoy the torment, and vainly tries to engage Madeline in more rational conversation. The narrator remarks caustically of Arabin after Madeline has played with him: 'This teacher of men, this Oxford pundit, this double-distilled quintessence of university perfection, this writer of religious treatises . . . had been like a little child in her hands . . . She could not but despise him for his facile openness, and yet she liked him for it too' (p. 371). Madeline has read Arabin correctly, and appreciated his unique honesty, but she continues to bewilder and badger him, almost getting him 'to own his love for Mrs Bold, and had subsequently almost induced him to acknowledge a passion for herself' (p. 394).

Arabin meanwhile is unconsciously making his own way with Eleanor who, after her trying day at Ullathorne, would hate him 'if she could' for hanging 'over that Italian woman as though there had been no beauty in the world but hers' (p. 425). That 'Italian woman', as we have seen, changes Eleanor's life, though the next time that Eleanor and Arabin are together he is foolish enough to talk of the signora's beauty. Arabin consistently continues to find it difficult to broach the subject of love. When he does apologize to her we note the dignified humility, and when he does, at last, utter his love we note the simplicity of the utterance. There are no sentences, no pat phrases, just 'Eleanor, my own Eleanor, my own, my wife!' (p. 466). It is fitting to leave Arabin at his moment of supreme happiness. The man of public words has become the man of strong private feeling. Trollope's ability to show character in development and undergoing change is nowhere better in evidence than in Mr Arabin, who enters the novel as the celibate fellow of an Oxford college, and leaves it as a man rendered warmer and more sympathetic – in effect, more human – by the giving and receiving of personal love. I suggest that he is ennobled, as well as fulfilled, by the tremulous nature of the experience.

Most of the characters in *Barchester Towers* participate in particular

Trollopian themes. Marriage, for instance, takes on contrasting forms: the balance of power within the Grantlys' marriage can be compared to the balance – or rather imbalance – within the Proudies'. Mrs Proudie rules her marriage openly, whereas Susan Grantly confines her influence to the bed-chamber. The bishop is ruled by Mrs Proudie in the home, and yet is presented as a competent committee man of acceptable opinions. In truth, the prelatess takes the decisions for which the bishop is held responsible, and we survey him in the light of this subservience. The publisher's reader of *Barchester Towers* considered that there was never any bishop like this one. Nevertheless, Trollope's portrait of this marriage remains convincing, and illustrates one all-embracing theme of the novel: clergymen are mere mortals. Trollope writes masterfully of romantic love but, in my view, is at his best when recording the reality of habit.

Mr and Miss Thorne

Another important theme emerges in the characterization of Mr and Miss Thorne: that of tradition. Trollope treats the eccentricities and idiosyncrasies of these two very much in the humorous vein he employs with considerable verve throughout the narrative. Wilfred Thorne, expert on genealogy, ultra-conscious of status, a bachelor with many prejudices, should be, like Sir Walter Elliot in *Persuasion*, a figure of fun. He certainly is to those contemporaries who see him in London trying to appear as a great man. An 'unflinching' conservative, he learns a broader tolerance; a sportsman, he gives up hunting because of political disagreements, but later returns to it. Trollope's comment is both humorous and ironic: 'But in hunting as in other things he was only supported by an inward feeling of mystic superiority to those with whom he shared the common breath of outer life' (p. 194).

Miss Thorne is just as strongly individualistic, just as rooted in the past ('She spoke of Addison, Swift, and Steele, as though they were still living', p. 194). Her genealogical passion almost outdoes her brother's, and her face is set against change or any modern political manifestation, such as democracy, the first Reform Bill of 1832 or the Bill of Catholic Emancipation (1829). She is a 'pure Druidess' (p. 195), and looks back to the 'divine right of kings as the ruling axiom of a golden age' (p. 196). Certainly the Thorne house suits their idiosyncrasies. Miss Thorne is lovable. She is 'a dear good odd creature . . . always glad to revert to anything' who 'would doubtless in time have reflected that fingers were made before forks, and have reverted accordingly' (p. 200). Mr Thorne has a function in the plot, notably to demonstrate that one is never too old to become ensnared in Madeline's ever-cast net. Miss Thorne is functional too, for she is determined to influence Eleanor in his direction by praising Mr Arabin.

In his preface to the Penguin edition J. K. Galbraith has called *Barchester Towers* 'a novel of politics, here between the two parties of the diocese and the cloister.' This conflict is, I think, evident, but as well as embracing opposition between High and Low church, it also embraces differences of class and status, which are recurring themes in most of Trollope's novels and particularly so in *Barchester Towers.* Take, for instance, the position of Slope who was a sizar at Cambridge and had university pupils. To Mrs Proudie, to the archdeacon, to Eleanor and to the bishop it is apparent that Slope lacks the qualifications (or perhaps just the qualities) to be considered a gentleman. Trollope, in his authorial persona, establishes Slope's suspect moral (and physical) hygiene: 'I never could endure to shake hands with Mr Slope' (p. 25). The gradations of class difference run throughout the novel with a certain structural balance. Dr Proudie is not the born gentleman in the sense that Dr Grantly is or, despite his moral and ecclesiastical irresponsibility, that Dr Vesey Stanhope is. Trollope is adept here at indicating the natural royalty of good breeding and its pre-eminence in society. Low Church may be equated with low breeding, and its antithesis is inheritance, tradition, rank.

The gathering at Ullathorne is illustrative of the differences. The careful presentation and interaction of Lookalofts and Greenacres (note the descriptive Dickensian names and the satirical tone) shows Trollope tracing class differences and aspirations amongst a lower stratum of society than that with which he generally deals. Yet in a sense this level mirrors the antagonisms of the upper. These 'outer classes' are part of Miss Thorne's patronage, and her provision for them unfortunately, if inadvertently, leads to conflict. We are told that 'Mrs Lookaloft's rise in the world had been wormwood to Mrs Greenacre' (p. 373). The humour here highlights the sense of class consciousness.

Despite her different vernacular, Mrs Greenacre feels in the same way here as the archdeacon does towards the usurping and ambitious Mr Slope. Galbraith refers to the chaplain as 'one of the most disastrous political operators of all time'. In practical terms this is not true, for Slope gets the widow and doubtless the money for a successful career. What he does not do is to succeed in breaking through the barrier of rigid class structure. But Slope is – and this too is a Trollopian theme – the indicator of change. For just as Trollope shows character developing and changing, so he shows the changes in society itself. The fact that Barchester has a Low Church bishop is itself indicative of change.

This long section has been concerned with character in action and the thematic nature of Trollope's writing in *Barchester Towers*. Trollope is a moral writer. This does not mean that he saw things as either black or white. It is one of his great virtues that he didn't, and that his wide knowledge of behaviour and perception of motives is evident on every page. He saw clearly the value of integrity, the strivings of ambition, the nature of power, the qualities of tradition, the inevitability of change, the virtue of humility, good breeding, kindliness and a whole range of themes which are reflected in the actions and interactions of character. What we see most forcibly in *Barchester Towers* is that Trollope's characters, like characters in life, are subject to change, to influence, to discovering more about themselves as new situations arise. It is this clarity of perception, this ability to weigh and display for the reader's judgement, which makes Trollope a good and sometimes great novelist.

5. Scenes and Settings

Scenes

Trollope commands a range of scenes, or dramatic action, which embrace the pathetic and the comic though not, as critics have been quick to point out, the tragic. The novel opens with a most effective scene, with the archdeacon and Mr Harding in attendance on the dying bishop. Such a scene focuses our attention at once, since on this death hangs, so to speak, the plot of the forthcoming novel. With the bishop's death comes action and reaction, movement, the sending of the telegram, the change of mood. From this opening the novel radiates out into a series of scenes of a widely contrasting nature.

If we have not met the archdeacon in *The Warden* we might take the opening scene as showing the nature of the man. It does not do so fully, for 'A Morning Visit' contains a set piece which provokes the 'war' of the following chapter. The 'scene' is set, but an addition which the archdeacon and Mr Harding do not expect takes the form of Mrs Proudie seated on the sofa (the sofa being the scene of her humiliation by Bertie later in the novel). Trollope's commentary on the initial power struggle ('There were four persons there, each of whom considered himself the most important person in the diocese; himself, indeed, or herself . . .' p. 31), provides the charge for the explosives. The scene is fraught with the archdeacon's suppressed anger, Mr Slope's impudence, Mrs Proudie's domination, the bishop's echo and Mr Harding's bewildered embarrassment.

Geoffrey Harvey has pointed out that Trollope read and annotated 257 early plays and has demonstrated his addiction to the Jacobean drama: certainly his sense of the dramatic, even melodramatic or comic-dramatic, is conveyed in his scenes, and the one which follows this neatly balances the private reactions of the archdeacon with the public performance of Slope in his provocative sermon. The sense of the dramatic is implicit in both, if different in kind. Take the archdeacon's vituperative 'like him!' which Trollope undercuts humorously by jingle verse: 'The old bells of the tower, in chiming the hour, echoed the words; and the swallows flying out from their nests mutely expressed a similar opinion' (p. 37). The effect is that of mild ridicule, the explosion is contained by a purgative laughter. This is the private anger of a public man, and the next scene shows this public man usurped by another who has mounted the pulpit of the cathedral. Trollope's method is admirable, for with Slope's sermon the anger becomes widespread, public (notice how quickly the bishop leaves Barchester in order to escape the immediate ecclesiastical row). The scene, as the audience takes in what Slope is saying, is dramatic in its general effect, but it is also, as so often in Trollope, personalized through an individual response, here that of the archdeacon. 'Then up rose Dr Grantly' (a parody, as U. C. Knoepflmacher points out, of Milton's *Paradise Lost*) opens the meeting – the public scene – which establishes the divisions or, to use the imagery of the novel, the declaration of war.

The above scene is a mixture of comedy with an underlying seriousness. 'Mrs Proudie's Reception' runs the gamut of comedy from wit to farce, with the aid of the sensual signora and the irrepressible Bertie Stanhope. There is a setting of the scene, the rooms being 'really very magnificent, or at least would be so by candlelight; and they had nevertheless been got up with commendable economy' (p. 78). Madeline's eruption into this – the waiting period having been filled in with conversation about her having 'no legs' – is preceded by a mock-heroic list of guests, the gathering of the guests in groups, and a general air of expectation. Her entry is dramatic, the cortège nearly knocks down Slope, and Madeline, having established whether the sofa is a right- or left-hand one, is dressed accordingly. Madeline on the sofa is deliberately associated in Trollope's description with Shakespeare's Cleopatra in the barge (*Antony and Cleopatra*, Act II, scene 2). I give the full passage here to show firstly that he is using the art of loose parody to achieve a comic-dramatic effect and, secondly, to show how the scene is calculatedly focused on the person who is to dominate it:

And very becoming her dress was. It was white velvet, without any other garniture than rich white lace worked with pearls across her bosom, and the same round the armlets of her dress. Across her brow she wore a band of red velvet, on the centre of which shone a magnificent Cupid in mosaic, the tints of whose wings were of the most lovely azure, and the colour of his chubby cheeks the clearest pink. On the one arm which her position required her to expose she wore three magnificent bracelets, each of different stones. Beneath her on the sofa, and over the cushion and head of it, was spread a crimson silk mantle or shawl, which went under her whole body and concealed her feet. Dressed as she was and looking as she did, so beautiful and yet so motionless, with the pure brilliancy of her white dress brought out and strengthened by the colour beneath it, with that lovely head and those large, bold, bright, staring eyes, it was impossible that either man or woman should do other than look at her. (p. 81)

The siren settles, and proceeds to unsettle, from this position; Bertie in 'light blue from head to foot' (p. 82) uses his mobility to overturn a number of conversations. But the centrepiece of the scene, and of the comic action, is the sofa, with Mrs Proudie cast as hostess and victim. Geoffrey Harvey has described the effect neatly when he says 'it is as though the sofa has obeyed the collective will of the assembly in order to prick her arrogance' (*The Art of Anthony Trollope*, p. 44). It is worth noticing how Trollope the narrator moves about the scene like one of the guests, thus creating the effect of being amidst the scene itself, tracing the group interaction. The climax of the scene is the pushing of the sofa into Mrs Proudie's lace train to the accompaniment of mock-epic similes, classical comparisons in the same vein, Madeline's comment followed by Bertie's imploring and exaggerated posturing and Mrs Proudie's exclamation from some 'scrap of dramatic poetry' (p. 85). The scene is punctuated with laughter – from the signora, and, at the expense of the fat rector, from Bertie.

Trollope's scenes are sometimes superbly visual, and this is no exception. The 'wide ruins of her magnificence' gathered up, Mrs Proudie's retreat is not without dignity as the 'girls fell into circular rank behind their mother, and thus following her and carrying out the fragments, they left the reception rooms' (p. 86), but the humour of the image is not lost upon the reader. The scene is far from over. The signora immediately engrosses the bishop, tells him her sad story, asks a personal blessing for 'the last of the Neros' (p. 87), while Bertie condemns Oxford and reveals himself as a one-time convert of the Jews. We note that there is no anti-climax after the sofa incident, and that an important plot pivot is used in the exchanges between Mr Harding and the bishop, and another in Slope's increasing attentions to Madeline, noticed and condemned by Mrs Proudie. Just as in a later setting at Ullathorne – which will be discussed later – one scene becomes several effective smaller scenes.

In contrast with this public scene, which gathers a large number of people together, are the more intimate dramas in which we witness the anger of the archdeacon, the ingratiations of Slope or, for example, the romance of Eleanor and Arabin. The first meeting between Slope and Harding is a notable scene. Harding is largely silent while Slope, with the intention of humiliating the man, expends his energy in rhetoric. Silence does not mean consent, however, and Slope overreaches himself. Although Harding is humiliated, the contrast between the two men, the genuine Christianity of the one and the obvious manipulative hypocrisy of the other, is effectively brought out. The scene reveals Slope's capacity for error and Harding's capacity for suffering. Related to this scene are Slope's interviews with Quiverful. Each shows us the slippery nature of the man. He first promises Quiverful the hospital, learns of Eleanor's fortune, and then retracts his offer by asserting that he didn't make it. These small scenes supplement the larger ones, for example the confrontation on just this issue between Slope, the bishop and Mrs Proudie, of which more later.

Slope's confrontation with Mrs Proudie is one of the major scenes of the novel. Mrs Proudie visits Slope in order to put him in his place, and we glimpse the coming eruption. The Stanhope scene, with Eleanor and Bertie together and the signora engrossing Slope, shows the dexterity with which Trollope is moving towards the climax. He is deliberately building up expectation and co-ordinating the plot elements leading to it. There is the retrospective view on Arabin, followed by Arabin and Eleanor in a scene important in terms of developing their own respect and feeling for each other.

Slope's visit to Puddingdale sparks off the now inevitable conflict. His scene with Mr Quiverful shows him at his manipulatory best (or worst), since he employs dishonesty and moral blackmail in order to make Quiverful feel that he himself has been wrong. Slope asserts his power in what is, for him, a small matter, almost as preface to asserting it on a much larger issue. But matters now move quickly. Mrs Quiverful has a scene with her husband indicating her own courage, and then a scene with Mrs Proudie which invites that lady's assistance and anger. The climatic scene is at hand, and Trollope introduces it with the tellingly brief: 'There was a dead pause in the room' (p. 231).

Mrs Proudie charges and is repulsed, knowing that later she will win, though this is small comfort now. The commentary balances the dialogue, with the bishop twiddling his thumbs and turning his eyes from one combatant to the other. The war imagery characterizes the exchanges. It is over as quickly as it began, but although we leave Slope and the bishop in charge of the field, another scene succeeds which is just as interesting. Trollope is adept at maintaining narrative interest. Here it lies in the fact that although Mrs Proudie has been defeated, and although in her initial frustration she upbraids Mrs Quiverful for her weak husband, she shows the lady kindness and humanity. It is the first time in the novel that we see her practical Christianity in action.

The scene between Madeline and Slope in which he professes his love, and she baits him mercilessly on his ambition and then points out at just the right moment that her husband is still living, shows Trollope bringing the triumphant Slope (after his victory over Mrs Proudie) down to earth.

In terms of timing it is incisively done, with Slope as the 'cockchafer' whirling round upon the signora's pin. The description of the scene has the signora with her writing-table before her, 'a barrier, as it were, against the enemy' (p. 247). 'She was sitting as nearly upright as she ever did', and both desk and position are important, since they indicate, firstly, that despite all her teasing she does keep her distance, while the uprightness signals the straight-talking rebuffs which she now administers to Slope. This scene anticipates her later directness in her scenes with Eleanor and with Arabin.

Trollope's balance between narrative flow, commentary and scene building shows an awareness of structure and plot and, more particularly, of reader involvement. Together with a variety of narrative styles we now have variety of scenes, moving from Mrs Proudie and Mrs Quiverful to Slope and Madeline and now to Eleanor and her scenes at Plumstead. As always, Trollope tends to use these scenes to mirror each other, so that there is a scene of recrimination with Mrs Grantly, one of a much softer nature with Mr Harding, then an angry and humiliating one with the archdeacon, and finally one of anger, frustration and misunderstanding with Mr Arabin. The progression in the above sequence will be noted. Although she is plagued by doubt, Eleanor adheres obstinately to her one misguided stance. Each scene reveals character and the force of the spoken word. Eleanor, the archdeacon and Arabin are passionate, the first because she has been wronged, the second because he is appalled and angry at what appears to be, and the third because he does not know how he is guilty of calumny, and also because he is in love and does not know it. The words show us the character at the moment of crisis and the scene demonstrates the character in action at that moment of crisis.

With the news of the dean's fatal illness there follow several interpolatory scenes, such as that between the bishop and Slope when the latter reveals that he has his own eye on the deanery. This is supplemented by a short scene in which Mrs Proudie puts down the bishop for even entertaining the idea that Slope might be considered for the deanery, and an even shorter scene in which Tom Staple puts forward the idea that the government might offer it to Mr Harding.

The Ullathorne *Fête Champêtre* is examined in more detail later, but here I want to consider the various scenes, of which this is one, which discerning critics have noted as the centrepiece of the novel. For the characters they all have serious consequences, but each of them is, I suggest, comic, and testifies to the variety of Trollope's comic art. In the *Fête Champêtre* there is, for example, the natural comic interaction between Miss Thorne, anxious for all to go well, and her steward Mr Plomacy, who has many fears and little tact with his mistress ('Bless your soul, ma'am . . . there won't be no old ladies, not one, barring yourself and old Mrs Clantantrum' (p. 332). There is further comic exchange between brother and sister over the quintain and the Beelzebub colt, and the social aspiration scene between the Lookalofts and Miss Thorne. As with Mrs Proudie's reception, Trollope is employing a similar technique – moving from group to group, though the initial centre is, as is fitting, the hostess. Again the author's tone is mock-epic, even mock-tragic, with a Greek chorus commenting on Harry Greenacre's accident.

Comedy gives way to abrupt and dramatic revelation when Eleanor, having been helped out of the carriage by Slope, relieves her father's worries by announcing her detestation of the chaplain. Her father enjoys his secret knowledge, not yet to be shared with the archdeacon. Mention of the latter, however, calls forth Eleanor's passion. The spirit she is to show later in the day is quickly in evidence when she accuses Dr Grantly (to her father) of 'traducing his sister-in-law and creating bitterness between a father and his daughter!' (p. 348). This is the first of the scenes in which Eleanor finds herself angered. Typically, by the end of their exchange, she has softened and is clinging to her father's arm.

The interaction between the signora, Lady De Courcy and Mrs Proudie is among the finest of the comic sequences in the novel. These are the main actresses, but there is a supporting cast, with the Honourable John eyeing the signora through his glass ('I have heard no end of stories about that filly', p. 351). Lady De Courcy makes Miss Thorne feel apologetic although there is nothing to be apologetic about, but there is an effective silent scene in which the countess loses a staring-out match with Madeline. The latter repeats her trick of the Proudie reception, making sure that Lady De Courcy hears what she says as she leaves. This is a consummate way of denigrating a woman whose attitudes denigrate others.

But Madeline is not centre stage in the comic interchange that follows, except as the subject for gossip and abuse. Mrs Proudie and Lady De Courcy get along famously, and Trollope's satirical thrusts at society at play are achieved through dialogue and reaction. Having verbally mutilated Miss Thorne, the ladies shred the signora. The 'ohs' and 'ahs' are expressive of the countess's joyful reception of what she is hearing. The scene depends for its effect on the quality of the dialogue and its implications:

'She's an abominable woman, at any rate,' said Mrs Proudie.
'Insufferable,' said the countess.

'She made her way into the palace once, before I knew anything about her; and I cannot tell you how dreadfully indecent her conduct was.'

'Was it?' said the delighted countess.

'Insufferable,' said the prelatess.

'But why does she lie on a sofa?' asked Lady De Courcy.

'She has only one leg,' replied Mrs Proudie.

'Only one leg!' said Lady De Courcy, who felt to a certain degree dissatisfied that the signora was thus incapacitated. 'Was she born so?'

'Oh no,' said Mrs Proudie – and her ladyship felt somewhat recomforted by the assurance – 'she had two. But that Signor Neroni beat her, I believe, till she was obliged to have one amputated. At any rate, she entirely lost the use of it.'

'Unfortunate creature!' said the countess, who herself knew something of matrimonial trials. (p. 355)

This kind of exchange needs to be given in some fullness because it shows the subtlety of Trollope's comic art. The dialogue says more than the words and the commentary. The last sentence quoted above, for example, is an oblique insight into character. There is a delightful verbal balancing in the scene (countess, prelatess) which corresponds to the natural agreement between two women of status discussing another. There is the exclamatory repetition (insufferable) and the relishing comedy of the leg. The scene between 'these congenial souls' is followed by another scene in which Mr Thorne, captivated by the signora, falls in love with her virtually at first sight. Trollope shifts again from this romantic comedy to a series of miniatures, chief among them being the archdeacon's endurance of Mrs Clantantram's attentions for the length of the banquet or Mr Arabin hanging 'enraptured and alone' (p. 360) over the signora's sofa.

The latter is explored in some detail, for Madeline 'read the secrets of his heart' (p. 365). She first of all baits him with the prospect of Eleanor and then finds that she is dealing with a man whose integrity is such that he only speaks the truth. The tensions are relieved by more rustic scenes, with Farmer Greenacre, Mrs Guffern and Mr Plomacy being the most prominent, the last-named exercising his functions of 'head constable as well as master of the revels' (p. 376).

Rustic slapstick is complemented by 'the quality in the tent on the lawn' (p. 379) and the speechmaking. Trollope's method is to traverse the social scene before returning to the particular which, in this case, proves to be the champagne-confident Slope's proposal to Eleanor. The jockeying for position, both physical and verbal, partakes of farce, with Slope being forced into his speech and insensitive to the discouragement he has received. His expression of love is as strong as that he had earlier offered Madeline, and the scene is enhanced by the sardonic authorial asides: '"Next to my hope of heaven are my hopes of possessing you." (Mr Slope's memory here played him false, or he would not have omitted the deanery)' (p. 383).

The parenthesis effectively conveys, of course, that Slope always plays false. The climax is the slap, but Trollope does not leave it at that. After Eleanor has escaped saying that she will never speak to Slope again, the chaplain licks his wounds in solitude but quickly surfaces when he sees the bishop in conversation with Dr Gwynne. He thrusts himself forward to get their notice, then quickly hastens away as the scene ends with the news of the dean's death.

The irony which attends most scenes in this variously comic novel is certainly present when Eleanor confides Slope's proposal to Charlotte who, after all, has played as falsely as Slope and is at this moment using Eleanor. She even suggests to Eleanor that perhaps Bertie should speak to Slope (Charlotte is certainly not slow to seize a chance which might further their cause) and then proceeds to make sure that Bertie has every opportunity to win Eleanor. That scene – we might accurately call it, I think, a non-proposal scene – again shows Trollope employing variety and contrast, Bertie the unready following Slope the importunate. Eleanor's scenes at Ullathorne show her passing through various degrees of frustration before she is to taste the joy of loving and being loved.

A touching scene, itself not without humour, finds the Quiverful family receiving the news of his appointment to the hospital. A scene which anticipates, in some ways, the one which brings Mrs Proudie down in *The Last Chronicle*, shows her displaying her prelatical powers in front of Dr Gwynne, who is appalled at her impudence. However she is still very much in control of the bishop at this stage. Eleanor worships her son as a reaction to what she has gone through and in front of her attendant, Mary Bold, invites her father to live with her, a further indication of her unsettled state. As one would expect in a novel nearing its close, certain scenes integral to the dénouement have to be played out.

After a Stanhope family scene in which Bertie is given his marching orders but has his debts settled, there is one of the climactic scenes of the novel. This is when Madeline tells Eleanor the state of her (Eleanor's) heart, and also the state of Mr Arabin's. It is done with high art, and we note the consistency of the characterization. Eleanor is understandably overcome after her experiences, while Madeline is more confident and assertive than ever, secure in the knowledge that what she is doing, *for once*, is right. She does it with powerful expedition and forthrightness, and although Eleanor gives her hand a squeeze, the naturalness of the scene is enhanced by the fact that we know Eleanor could never like Madeline and that Madeline feels something like contempt for the conventional woman she knows Eleanor to be.

The signora goes on to a greater triumph. Her scene with Slope, Arabin and Mr Thorne reflects her abilities to manoeuvre and shows, too, the quality of heartlessness (note the contrast with the previous scene) which Trollope stressed in his earlier account of the family. Slope is once more the cockchafer on the pin, and she delights in the torture. There is a kind of black comedy in this, for the laughter is demonic. Dramatically it is a fine scene, a fitting farewell for the signora, whose intelligence, wit, sensuality and unscrupulousness have dominated throughout.

After the signora's triumph. it is only right that Mr Harding should have his, and who more pleasant to score off and to reassure at the same time than the archdeacon? His first card is the offer of the deanery, which he intends to turn down; his second is not played until he learns that Eleanor is to marry Arabin, while his third arises from this, when he determines to yield up the deanery to his future son-in-law. There is, so to speak, a scale of surprises for the archdeacon in these scenes, his relief and pleasure later expended in his material generosity. After the first scene we have the coming together of Arabin and Eleanor. Here Trollope shows his control and understanding of the emotional interaction between two people who have been at the crossroads of misunderstanding for too long. The result is Arabin's simple claiming of Eleanor as his wife, her breaking away from him in her extremity of happiness, and her returning impetuously to hand him her child; when she stoops to take him back, she 'kissed the hand that held him' (p. 467). It is one of the most natural love scenes in fiction, the characters of Eleanor and Arabin revealed, by their reactions and their delight in each other, in complete compatibility.

Dramatic interaction continues, Mr Harding telling his daughter of the offer of the deanery, and Eleanor confiding that she is to be married 'if you will approve' (p. 472). He does, and has his second little triumph when he tells the archdeacon. The latter's generosity extends to the Quiverfuls – at least in terms of manner and mood – since the old order by which he has lived is not going to change. The situation has been well put by David Skilton when he describes *Barchester Towers* as 'a conservative comedy, in both senses of that expression: at once restoring the old order by the expulsion of the intruder, and expressing a victory for social and political conservatism' (*Introduction to 'Barchester Towers',*

p. 9). The irony is that Slope is expelled by his own party in the shape of Mrs Proudie playing the part of bishop for the last time in the novel. The scene reflects her splenetic nature, her sexual jealousy, her capacity for and indulgence of revenge. Again the contrast with the previous scenes of happiness, love, reconciliation, is marked. The convention of the happy ending for the fictional illusion must be maintained, and is perhaps symbolized by the scene in which Mr Harding accompanies Quiverful arm-in-arm when he takes over the wardenships.

For Trollope, the scene is the pivot of his narrative, whether it be crowded or intimate, dramatic or comic, poignant or joyful: and he demonstrates, time and time again, variety, control, feeling for character in action and reaction and, in greater degree than he is often given credit for, an awareness of artistic effect.

Settings

Scenes require settings, and we note that the first scene of the novel is set in the palace. Trollope makes use of the palace setting on a number of contrasting occasions. This first one invokes the past, with the old bishop in benign rule, the archdeacon powerful and assertive, Mr Harding in attendance on his old friend to the last. But the register of change is inexorable. When the archdeacon and Mr Harding call to see the new bishop they 'were shown through the accustomed hall into the well-known room, where the good old bishop used to sit. The furniture had been bought at a valuation, and every chair and table, every bookshelf against the wall, and every square in the carpet, was as well known to each of them as their own bedrooms. Nevertheless they at once felt that they were strangers there. The furniture was for the most part the same, yet the place had been metamorphosed. 'A new sofa had been introduced, a horrid chintz affair . . .' (p. 29). Here the setting is symbolic, and the description preludes spoken words which are going to underline the change. Mention of the sofa anticipates the comedy at Mrs Proudie's reception. The setting itself is part of the change: 'No company had been seen in the palace since heaven knows when' (p. 77). Mrs Proudie organizes her suite of rooms and the palace becomes social centre and theatre of war at one and the same time.

The importance of setting in these two chapters cannot be overstressed. The first thing which one would associate with the episcopal palace is, I suppose, formal Christianity. That is certainly not present here – in other words the setting serves ironically as comment on divisions, not only ecclesiastical divisions but social and moral ones as well. The cheap wine is an ironic comment on Mrs Proudie's (Low Church and sabbatarian) preparation of the reception, where intruders (Madeline and Bertie) usurp what is a most serious occasion for the official providers (the bishop and his wife). By using the palace as the setting on a number of occasions Trollope manages to make it, comically for the most part, a centre of strife, such as the reception in the humiliation of Mrs Proudie, but later in scenes as various as Slope's interview with Harding about the wardenship, his winning the battle against Mrs Proudie over the Quiverful appointment, Mrs Quiverful's interviews with Mrs Proudie, and so on. The disintegration of the Slope–Proudie alliance in that final momentous interview when Slope looks at Mrs Proudie 'with a very heavenly look' (p. 486) rounds off the palace settings.

The interior settings are for the most part not given much physical detail, but they are given physical presence and atmosphere, as in the comfortable parsonage at Plumstead Episcopi and the contrasting poverty of the Quiverful home. There is an interesting, even meaningful investigation of St Ewold's, with the archdeacon's authority stamped on the changes he would make in every room, and even a battle over a round table. We spend some time at the Stanhopes, more at Plumstead, and we visit Eleanor. At the back of the Barchester settings there looms, though without specific description, the London setting, with Dr Proudie finally taking his seat in the House of Lords, and the Oxford setting, High Church headquarters which is going to influence the appointment to the deanery. The outstanding setting, and it stands in contradistinction to that of the palace, is Ullathorne. There the old and the new meet, and there the major decisions of the characters are taken. As James Kincaid has put it, 'The party, apparently a monstrous ritual of dedication to illusion and the dead, becomes the scene for clarity and rejuvenation' (*Introduction to 'Barchester Towers'*, p. xviii).

Mr Thorne's house is based on Montacute House near Yeovil in Somerset. Trollope wrote of it: 'But for colour of stone, irregularity of design falling into and creating lines of architectural beauty, and for general picturesque forms of stonework without such magnificence as that of Longleat or Hatfield, Montacute House is the best example I know in England' (*Letters* I, 333). Trollope describes the interior of Ullathorne in great detail, but then tells the reader that it is 'the outside of Ullathorne that is so lovely' (p. 201). Significantly, the chapter ends with the following statements: 'Such a year or two since were the Thornes of Ullathorne. Such, we believe, are the inhabitants of many an English country home. May it be long before their number diminishes' (p. 202).

Ullathorne represents Trollope's love of tradition – eccentricities and all – but it also represents his acknowledgement of change.

The setting somehow brings out the deeper feelings in people (if we accept that Slope has feelings that are not motivated by ambition), so that the signora and Bertie, for instance, behave better than they expected to themselves or than we expected them to. Eleanor and Arabin discover themselves, and Mr Thorne falls in love. Miss Thorne helps Eleanor to recognize her own love, while the games themselves (Trollope's own parody of the Earl of Eglinton's medieval tournament held in 1839) convey something of the past in terms of feudal spirit. The *fête champêtre* is itself a microcosm of ecclesiastical and secular society, with the setting providing a kind of catalyst. What is finely conveyed is the sense of space. Although the Lady De Courcy complains about the roads, there is little doubt that her journey has been worthwhile for the benefit of Mrs Proudie's gossip. The aspirations of Lookalofts and Greenacres are seen against the background of a setting they can visit but never reach. For if things are resolved at Ullathorne, the permanence of their resolution is weighed against the permanence of a society, epitomized by the place.

6. Style and Narrative

Trollope's style has been the subject of much critical debate. Geoffrey Tillotson considered it 'a style for all purposes, being capable of handling the trivial and commonplace, and also the noble and splendid' (*Mid-Victorian Studies*, p. 60). John W. Clark said that 'Trollope's normal style is remarkably uniform, from beginning to end; uniformly easy, flowing, clear, plain, unlaboured, unaffected, unmannered, and above all businesslike' (*The Language and Style of Anthony Trollope*, p. 19). These are large but justifiable claims, and Clark goes on to note, among other things, the variety of tone from the waggish to the solemn, and how Trollope often writes in balanced sentences, or with pairs of sentences balancing each other. Clark's book is invaluable for the student of Trollope, since it indicates archaic usages (such as Slope's remark of the dying dean that 'his intellects cannot possibly survive it', p. 298), disagreements in number, and confusion, for example, between 'lie' and 'lay'. It also covers contemporary usages such as Charlotte referring to her father as the 'governor', and the rare moment when the archdeacon calls his wife 'Sue' when he has just heard that Eleanor is to marry Arabin ('He did not call his wife Sue above twice or thrice in a year, and these occasions were great high days' p. 480). *Barchester Towers* has the additional stylistic effect of dialect (particularly in chapter 5 of the third volume), for example, Mrs Guffern in full flow: 'She told me she zee'd 'em come in – that they was dressed finer by half nor any of the family, with all their neckses and buzoms stark naked as a born baby' (p. 374). It is also part of Trollope's style to use suggestive names – like Mrs Greenacre, Mrs Lookaloft (sufficiently indicative of her ambitions) and more subtle ones, a kind of Greek joke, in Sir Lamda Mewnew and Sir Omicron Pie, playing on letters of the Greek alphabet. Of all his novels, *Barchester Towers* is perhaps the richest in its stylistic effects. This is largely because it is primarily a comic socio-romantic novel, and Trollope uses parody, allusion, mock-heroic, mock-epic, slang (Eleanor has plenty of 'tin' from Bertie's point of view) and a variety of other stylistic effects to bring out situation and character. Some of these will be examined below.

The omniscient voice

As Ruth apRoberts in *Trollope: Artist and Moralist* (Chatto and Windus, 1971) reminds us, Paul Elmer More expressed the view as far back as 1928 that Trollope's art is not at all weakened by authorial comment, but in fact is enhanced. That the novel is an illusion created through words is a constant reminder throughout Trollope's narrative. Having set in motion that part of the plot where Bertie is made to emerge as a suitor for Eleanor's hand, Trollope tells the reader 'It is not destined that Eleanor shall marry Mr Slope or Bertie Stanhope' (p. 126) and then qualifies his practice:

> Our doctrine is that the author and the reader should move along together in full confidence with each other. Let the personages of the drama undergo ever so completely a comedy of errors among themselves, but let the spectator never mistake the Syracusan for the Ephesian; otherwise he is one of the dupes, and the part of a dupe is never dignified. (p. 127)

Trollope, by confiding in the reader, is in effect taking the reader along with him on his own particular ride. Donald Smalley has put it well when he observed that in a Trollope novel there is 'the unifying play of the author's voice, the sense of a mind that experienced all this life and brought it all under the narrator's control, with a special quality of self-effacement that is sometimes taken for simple maladroitness' (*Trollope: The Critical Heritage*, p. 8). Trollope's tone here defines exactly what his fiction is, the shared experience of creator and reader. Sometimes the voice is almost self-mocking. Take the statement: 'We must beg to be allowed to draw a curtain over the sorrows of the archdeacon as he sat, sombre and sad at heart, in the study of his parsonage at Plumstead Episcopi' (p. 8). This is, indicated by the alliteration, a gentle satire of sentiment. Yet the novelist knows that he is going to present us with a different kind of sentiment – over Harding, over Eleanor, for example – during the course of his novel. This self-consciousness sometimes takes on a humorous contemporary dimension, as with 'a poor novelist when he attempts to rival Dickens or rise above Fitzjeames, commits no fault, though he may be foolish' (p. 8). All this is by way of apologizing for the archdeacon's worldly ambitions. The omniscient voice can take on a moral tone, but it can also display the broad-minded tolerance which is typical of Trollope's stance as a writer.

The ironic use of the voice embraces character and situation. The description of Slope is followed by: 'Think, oh, my meditative reader, what an associate we have here for those comfortable prebendaries, those gentleman-like clerical doctors, those happy, well-used, well-fed minor canons, who have grown into existence under the kindly wings of Bishop Grantly!' (p. 26). This is the Trollope who, while delighting in the good breeding and comfort he describes, yet has a converse delight in seeing that its disturbance may be salutary and challenging. The voice is also employed in extension of the mock-epic, mock-heroic tone which characterizes so much of the comic narrative in *Barchester Towers*. 'And now, had I the pen of a mighty poet, would I sing in epic verse the noble wrath of the archdeacon' (p. 36). The simulated voice is that of Homer at the opening of The *Iliad*, but the great deeds of the Greeks and Trojans are reflected in the distorted mirror of the small deeds of High and Low Church in Barchester. This kind of tone is brilliantly extended in 'The Dean and Chapter Take Counsel', where the various speakers, led by the archdeacon, who is wickedly cast in the Satan role, approximate to the debaters in Hell in Book II of *Paradise Lost*. This has been superbly charted by U. C. Knoepflmacher in his discussion of the novel in *Laughter and Despair in Ten Victorian Novels*.

The omniscient voice is not always devoted to humour, satire, mockery. Sometimes it is employed in a cynical appraisal of the nature of life:

> A man in the wrong knows that he must look to his weapons; his very weakness is his strength. The one is never prepared for combat, the other is always ready. Therefore it is that in this world the man that is in the wrong almost invariably conquers the man that is in the right, and invariably despises him. (p. 352)

This passage comes from *Barchester Towers* and concerns the putting down of Miss Thorne by Lady De Courcy and her daughter. In a novel in which the meek and good (Harding and Arabin) inherit the earth, Trollope also shows that the aristocratic and ill-bred inherit the earth too. It is a wise and balanced appraisal of human nature.

Some readers have found the self-consciousness of Trollope's voice annoying or cloying, but Trollope himself regarded fiction, in important ways, as an entertainment. The final chapter of *Barchester Towers* opens with the words 'The end of a novel, like the end of a children's dinner-party, must be made up of sweetmeats and sugar-plums' (p. 495). This statement is essentially Trollope's recognition of the boundaries of fictional convention, with its obligatory happy ending and a rounding off summary. Yet even here I feel that Trollope is not simply indulging in neat, almost throw-away asides which mock the convention and the statements he feels obliged to make. Thus he tells of Eleanor and Arabin answering 'I will', and then observes: 'We have no doubt that they will keep their promises; the more especially as the Signora Neroni had left Barchester before the ceremony was performed' (p. 495).

That kind of understated irony typifies so much of the authorial commentary in *Barchester Towers*. The voice is always engaging in its comments, whether it underlines the humour constructed within the novel, or whether it guides us out to the broad humour of life itself.

Dialogue and description

The evenness of Trollope's style is evident in his set-piece descriptions of people, places, and situations, while his dialogue is unforced and natural. With the exception of the dialect referred to earlier, the language is the civilized language of educated people. In many instances, so good is Trollope's ear, that the language is the man. Here is Mr Harding:

I can't say I felt myself much disposed to like him. (p. 38)

I don't suppose he can do us much harm. (p. 39)

I don't suppose Eleanor need call. I don't think Eleanor would get on at all well with Mrs Proudie. (p. 41)

The first two statements are about Slope, the last, of course, about Mrs Proudie. All three reflect Mr Harding's diffidence, his private nature, his wish to avoid friction, his attempts to be self-contained. A similar illustration could be given with the archdeacon, particularly when angered, and Arabin in rational expression, or Slope in smooth persuasion, or the bishop in indecision, or Mrs Proudie in denunciation, or the signora in manipulation. Bertie, too, is strongly individualized through his speech, and his remarks at Mrs Proudie's reception reflect his dilettante and irresponsible nature – though no one could accuse him of narrowness of interests.

Trollope is adept at the conversation interacting with his own commentary. When Susan Grantly goes to interrogate her sister about the letter she has received from Mr Slope, Eleanor's mounting anger is seen in the commentary which has her turning red, trying to keep her colour, failing to do so, feeling angry at being cross-examined, and determining not to tell her sister what is in the letter because she knows that she has been set on by the archdeacon.

Trollope's descriptions are admirably lucid, often balanced, brief in the direct impression, as in the death of the old bishop: 'There was no loud rattle in the throat, no dreadful struggle, no palpable sign of death;

but the lower jaw fell a little from its place, and the eyes which had been so constantly closed in sleep now remained fixed and open' (p. 4). Here the understatement has all the necessary finality. Sometimes the description, particularly when it has a retrospective angle, takes on a rhetorical flavour, but it is not inflated. The account of Arabin's life before we meet him is admirably economical, but conveys, through the repetitions, the dedication and the quality of the man:

> As a boy young Arabin took up the cudgels on the side of the Tractarians, and at Oxford he sat for a while at the feet of the great Newman. To this cause he lent all his faculties. For it he concocted verses, for it he made speeches, for it he scintillated the brightest sparks of his quiet wit. For it he ate and drank and dressed and had his being. (p. 169)

The control of tone here reflects the control Arabin himself exercises until Eleanor comes into his life, the prose even anticipating the man's own measured, balanced form of speech.

Retrospect

This brings me to a technique, the use of 'retrospect', much employed in *Barchester Towers* (though not so much elsewhere in Trollope). It is necessary in this novel since it is nominally a successor to *The Warden*. There is a very complete survey of relevant material up to 'A Morning Visit', three chapters being devoted progressively to Mr Harding and Hiram's Hospital and Eleanor Bold and her widowhood, followed by the career of Dr and Mrs Proudie, and finally of Mr Slope. In the latter's case Trollope is able to indulge himself in a literary joke ('I have heard it asserted that he is lineally descended from that eminent physician who assisted at the birth of Mr T. Shandy', p. 22) which prepares the way for caricature, although Slope is not simply this, having, as we have seen, some fullness.

That three chapters early in a novel should be weighted with the past is unusual, but here it is effective because it achieves the necessary integration into the action of the present – it prepares for war by establishing the reasons for it. After four chapters of action and reaction Trollope again refers to the past in order to bring into the foreground the Stanhope family, three of whom are to play important parts in the ensuing action involving the romantic and, up to a point, the ecclesiastical parts of the narrative. The main actors are almost all assembled by the end of the first volume, but others are to enter and influence, and Trollope employs precisely the same technique in each instance.

Volume II opens with a full account of Arabin's career which has the function of placing him in moral opposition to Slope, *and* of indicating his vulnerability through his temptation towards Rome. It also gives Trollope the opportunity to fill in more details of the religious background of the time.

But the retrospect on the Thornes, structurally and symbolically, is the most telling in the novel, for Ullathorne becomes the centre, as we have seen, for revelation and resolution. The account of Mr Thorne is of a confirmed conservative rooted in the past who confronts the powerful, almost irresistible influence for change in the signora, who masters him as she masters others. Miss Thorne's eccentricities and her love of the past, reflected in a literary taste which knows no present, has pathos as well as humour in it. Trollope tells us that she had lovers, and her nostalgia for the past acts on the present to help Eleanor get the right one.

Trollope's use of retrospect not only contributes to a leisurely narrative pace, but gives the author the opportunity to explore more deeply the social, moral and psychological aspects of the novel. I suggest, too, that Trollope is far from being the casual writer he would have us believe when he says in *An Autobiography*: 'When I sit down to write a novel I do not at all know, and I do not very much care, how it is to end.' One can only observe that he finds out very quickly and applies himself assiduously to the coherent artistic structure which characterizes the finished product.

Classical and literary references

John Clark has demonstrated the allusive quality of *Barchester Towers* with its 'multitude of literary allusions, quotations and echoes'. Again one has the feeling that the value of these – Clark traces seventy of them – is not merely ornamental, but serves the ironic, satirical or mock-heroic modes of narration. The classical references are almost always of a humorous bent. Take the first of these, and you will see the depth at which Trollope is working. In relation to Hiram's Hospital and the press campaign surrounding it he observes: 'But Cassandra was not believed, and even the wisdom of the *Jupiter* sometimes falls on deaf ears' (p. 11). In Virgil's *Aeneid* Cassandra was not believed, for instance, in her accurate warning about the wooden horse entering Troy, but the irony here lies in the fact that the *Jupiter* sets itself up to be all-seeing. Of course it is not – it sees only what its bias wants it to see.

Mrs Proudie's strict vigilance is conveyed by the description of her as having 'the eyes of Argus' (p. 21), a one-hundred-eyed giant, while the archdeacon, we are told, feels that 'Dr Proudie was playing Venus to his Juno' (p. 29). The effect of these references is to provide a subtext which in fact mocks misplaced seriousness or pretentiousness. One composite reference establishes a perspective on 'future wars of Arabin and Slope': the 'frogs and the mice would be nothing to them, nor the angers of Agamemnon and Achilles' (pp. 116–17). The quarrel between these two Greek warriors is related to the present squabble between Low-Church and High-Church but the reference here is comic, stressing that, while such may be a matter of life and death to the protagonists, it is not the stuff of the heroic epic.

Perhaps the fullest reference is to Mrs Quiverful as Medea (p. 221), in which Trollope elevates the prolific woman to the status of heroine as she fights for her children's future. And Trollope does here what he repeats two chapters later with the signora – he links the classical reference to a string of other literary associations, including Theseus's love for an amazon (Mrs Quiverful is certainly that), Lear's description of Cordelia, and one of the several quotations from *Macbeth* (see pp. 221–2). The very profusion of references here strengthens the irony by the *real* pathos of the Quiverfuls' situation. Some eight chapters later there is another Medea reference, and this time it is to a burlesque version which ran in a West End Theatre at the time that *Barchester Towers* was being written. Trollope observes that 'Mrs Proudie was the Medea of Barchester; she had no idea of not eating Mr Slope . . . she would pick him to the very last bone' (p. 316). It seems to me that by thus associating Mrs Quiverful and Mrs Proudie Trollope is using a delightful form of burlesque. Whether the situation subscribes to pathos or revenge, the parallels are so deliberately far-fetched so as to enhance the sense of the ridiculous.

Other literary references carry their own weight. The idea of the bishop reading the latest number of the '"*Little Dorrit*" of the day' (p. 411) is Trollope's admission of the compulsive power of Dickens, a mark of respect here which compares with his earlier sneers at Mr Popular Sentiment in *The Warden*. The reference to Disraeli's Sidonia (p. 70), the Jewish financier, is used to pinpoint the susceptibility of Bertie, who has been both converted and swindled. There is a nice ironic allusion to Mr Arabin's 'Wertherian grief' as he wanders about Plumstead 'an ancient love-lorn swain' (p. 318). Shakespeare references range from Petruchio (*The Taming of the Shrew*) to Imogen (*Cymbeline*) with, as I mentioned before, echoes from *Macbeth* such as when, before Slope proposes to Eleanor, he feels: 'That which has made them drunk, has made me bold'.

In fact it makes him foolish and misguided – and humiliated (see pp. 314, 245, 380 respectively). Other references run from Milton to Sir Henry Taylor's *Philip van Artevelde* (1834), while Madeline adapts to her own satirical satisfaction an old Scotch folk-song (p. 448) which enables her to send Mr Slope on his way. There is also the analogy with literary characters, such as the particularly apt modelling of Mr Thorne on Samuel Richardson's exemplary hero *Sir Charles Grandison* (1754). This fits exactly the description we have been given of the man who lives much of his life in the eighteenth century in spirit. Sometimes the quotation signals a departure, and not merely a physical one. Before Slope sees the bishop for the last time Trollope quotes the final lines of *Lycidas* (p. 483). These forecast Slope's state of mind and his future achievement. The 'fresh woods and pastures new' are in his case located in the vicinity of Baker Street.

Biblical references

As befits a struggle between ecclesiastical factions, the Bible is used as a source for commentary on their actions. Slope's name is Obadiah, a fitting irony since it is Hebrew for 'Lord's servant', which, applied to Slope, is dubious. Mrs Proudie always has Biblical reprimands to cite in support of her religiosity, as in: 'Neither thou, nor thy, nor thy daughter . . .' (p. 35). This is from the Ten Commandments (Exodus xx:10) but, delivered as interrogation and lecture to Mr Harding, its inappropriateness is a censure on Mrs Proudie's arrogant Sabbatarianism. Trollope has Slope take 2 Timothy ii:15 for his text when he preaches in the cathedral. The words are manipulated by Slope into an attack on those present, reflecting his own cunning and hypocrisy (remember that the bishop does not know what text Slope has chosen and is horrified as he sits through it). Later Slope is compared to St Paul's spiritual instructor Gamaliel, who taught Paul the exact observance of the laws of his ancestors. Slope's new-found power in Barchester is described with allusion to Christ's miracle when we are told that he has control of 'the loaves and fishes of the diocese of Barchester' (p. 49). He attracts those among the clergy who consider themselves needy and who see in Slope the possibility of relief and provision through advancement.

It would take too long to examine every one of Trollope's associations. They are generally weighted comments, and particularly effective on character. 'With the archdeacon it would have been the text for a rejoinder which would not have disgraced Bildad the Shuhite' (p. 427) is a somewhat esoteric reference to one of the most extreme of Job's comforters (one who responds to Job's suffering by rubbing salt into his wounds), yet the grandiloquence here adds all the more emphasis to the satire on Dr Grantly. Just as effective is the quotation comment on Slope's self-styled grandeur. Trollope cites Psalm 137: 'Precentors, vicars, and choristers might hang up their harps on the willows . . . the glory of their house was departing from them' (p. 442) to evoke a mock-pathos. Here, as elsewhere, these allusions highlight Trollope's particular brand of irony.

I am aware that in this section it is not possible to do full justice to Trollope's stylistic versatility. The urbane and even flow, the invocations, descriptions and dialogue which break it or change its course temporarily are all part of Trollope's natural and confiding style. An unsigned review in *The Leader* of 23 May 1857 referred to 'the astonishing energy with which the author writes, the sharpness and concision of his style, the light, unlaboured scatterings of allusions, the points that strike in all directions against the faces and follies of our ecclesiastical civilization . . .'. This underlines a great deal of Trollope's style. There is also a humanity and wisdom which permeates *Barchester Towers* and his other great novels. The ease of expression testifies to his own meticulous attention every morning to what he had written the day before, 'weighing with my ear the sound of the words and phrases'. Trollope's narrative blends discipline and imagination to produce the balance and the harmony which typify his best work.

Other aspects of style

Trollope uses a number of French and Latin terms, the latter sometimes of a legal nature. Chapter 17 has the author tinting his final pages *'couleur de rose'*, and he also has Slope vanquished by Mrs Proudie who is *'facile princeps'*. These tags lie lightly on the narrative. There is a range of contemporary references, most of which have to do with the immediate religious or historical background to *Barchester Towers*. The reference to 'all our examination tests' (p. 412) is a bitter little remark which reflects Trollope's dislike of competitive tests for the Civil Service which had recently (1854) been recommended by the Northcote–Trevelyan report. It also refers, I think, to *Little Dorrit*, where the Civil Service, dubbed the Circumlocution Office, had been under fire from Dickens.

There is some satire on the subject of the press, some satire on mock-tournaments, like the one at Ullathorne, and there is some use of contemporary slang terms which have already been referred to.

Trollope employs alliteration and antithesis, almost in an augustan way, as in 'to overlook what he had lost, and think only of what he might possibly gain' (p. 5). He uses rhetorical paragraphs, in which the use of repetition leading towards the climactic statement is a feature, as in: 'That same day, after dinner, Eleanor, with an assumed air of dignity which she could not maintain, with tears which she could not suppress, with a flutter which she could not conquer, and a joy which she could not hide, told Miss Thorne that she was engaged to marry Mr Arabin . . .' (p. 459).

Barchester Towers and Novels of its Time

Barchester Towers is the book which establishes Trollope as a major novelist, bringing him into the company of Dickens and Thackeray and a new, unknown writer called George Eliot, who published her *Scenes of Clerical Life* from January to November 1857 in *Blackwood's Edinburgh Magazine*. Charlotte Brontë was dead, and in 1857 Mrs Gaskell issued her life of the novelist, still a standard biography. Dickens's *Little Dorrit* was issued in monthly numbers from December 1855 until June 1857, and is therefore exactly contemporaneous with *Barchester Towers*. Thackeray had completed one of his greatest novels, *The Newcomes*, two years before *Barchester Towers*, and Mrs Gaskell had done the same with *North and South*. She did not produce another novel of note until *Sylvia's Lovers* (1863) while Thackeray, having toured America lecturing widely, began to issue *The Virginians* in 1857. It remains to be said that when *Barchester Towers* was issued in May 1857 Meredith had published his burlesque *The Shaving of Shagpat* (1856), favourably reviewed by George Eliot. In 1857 Henry James was fourteen years old, and Thomas Hardy was seventeen.

Trollope invites immediate comparison with Dickens through their social arenas are largely different, their social concerns certainly so, their methods markedly dissimilar. *Little Dorrit*, which shows Dickens at the height of his artistic and imaginative awareness, contains a scathing satire on the Civil Service, with 'how not to do it' as its major theme. It also contains a middle-aged hero in Arthur Clennam who shares a quality of diffidence with Mr Harding, but certainly nothing else. There is no single character in *Barchester Towers* who can rank with Mr Dorrit in terms of psychological investigation, consistency, emotional and mental breakdown, or with Mrs Clennam in like compass. Although *Barchester Towers* is a comic novel, there are no characters to equal the verbally importunate Flora, the verbally neutered Mrs General, or the verbally and physically frightening Mr F's aunt. And nowhere does Trollope get to the appraisal of a society which produces and worships a Mr Merdle.

Little Dorrit is one of the greatest Victorian novels because it exposes its own society to a terrible and searching scrutiny and concludes that it is a prison, one that is in a state of disintegration. Financiers and houses fall, ruining all and sundry; those who appear beneficent are corrupt and evil. A bankrupt with the longest service behaves as an aristocrat with the longest title; ideas are stifled, the good and well-meaning suffer, sincerity is a poor qualification beside opportunism. It is fitting that the bishop of Barchester should read the *Little Dorrit* of the day. Trollope may have disagreed with the attack on the Circumlocution Office, but the overall nature of the Dickensian assault is not dissimilar (except in tone) from some of Trollope's concerns in *The New Zealander*.

Yet there are areas in *Barchester Towers* where Trollope is seen to advantage. Although it could be argued that Slope smacks of caricature, there is nothing in Trollope's novel to compare with the one-dimensional and melodramatic Blandois/Rigaud, last seen smoking in the window of the house. He serves the complexity of the plot, with Dickens revealing all in the wonderful narrative speed, which has the habitually immobile Mrs Clennam hysterically taking up her skirts and running.

In *Barchester Towers* the handling of plot is superbly paced through action and interaction, by the authorial comment and direction, by the incisive focus on scene and setting. Dickens's plot is needlessly complex and concealed, while Trollope's onward movement is easy and natural. Because of the convention of informing the reader, for example, of what Eleanor will *not* do, Trollope sacrifices some (by no means all) tension, while Dickens maintains it through a series of dramatic strokes, some of them unexpected. And although Dickens does not tell us that Arthur Clennam will marry Amy, it is sufficiently obvious from very early in the narrative.

Trollope's irony which runs through *Barchester Towers*, directing its wit at faction, pretension, pride and snobbery, is not as insistently dark as the irony of *Little Dorrit*. The Marshalsea straddles the past and reaches into the present and beyond. The two book titles, 'Poverty' and 'Riches', carry their own unifying overtone, since, for example, the poverty of the first has a richness to be found in Amy Dorrit's dedication, while the riches of the second have the corresponding poverty of loss. We move into extremes, so that Clennam, providing testimonials for the Father of the Marshalsea, finds himself in the father's place needing only the testimonial of love. Such depths are not stirred by Trollope, and the economic deprivation of the Quiverfuls is imagined, rather than felt by the reader. Yet there are similarities between the two novels. Trollope takes a segment of society – largely the ecclesiastical – while Dickens ranges from debtors to millionaires, civil servants and politicians, social snobs like Mrs Gowan, and psychopaths like her son and Miss Wade. Dickens's imagination encompasses more than Trollope's, with its sense of the grotesque and its wonderful combination of both the oblique and the direct in the novel – the first being found in the meeting of the travellers in the mountains, the second in the mental collapse of Mr Dorrit as the past swamps his consciousness at the dinner in Rome. To read *Little Dorrit* is to touch imaginative greatness and artistic coherence at every turn of the narrative. Trollope, I believe, came somewhere near to the same achievement in *The Way We Live Now* (1875).

The Virginians (issued 1857–9) did little for Thackeray's contemporary reputation and has done less for his posthumous one. He had published *The History of Henry Esmond* in 1852, a work of profound historical evocation containing memorable characters such as Beatrix, Henry and Lady Castlewood. Esmond's marriage to the widowed Lady Castlewood disquieted many contemporary reviewers, but the novel was a great success and increased Thackeray's claim to be ranked alongside Dickens as the finest novelist of the age. *The Newcomes*, published 1853–5, shows Thackeray making use of his own Anglo-Indian background as well as of contemporary London, with its many corrupt and worldly associations. The novel achieves a pathetic climax with the death of Colonel Newcome, who had lost his fortune and been reduced to extreme poverty. As Ann Monsarrat has said, 'In *Esmond* he had brought to life a distant age. In *The Newcomes*, he preserved his own for posterity.' By the time he came to write *The Virginians* Thackeray's health had deteriorated. He suffered from stricture of the urethra and attacks of ague, but insisted on undertaking strenuous lecture tours. In addition to this he decided – as Trollope was to later – to stand as an independent liberal candidate in an election. He lost to Edward Cardwell, a future statesman of unquestionable ability, but he also lost a lot of money in electioneering expenses. It was largely to recoup this that he undertook *The Virginians*, a rambling book which describes the fortunes of the descendants of Colonel Henry Esmond. It is set in England and Virginia. Beatrix, now old, has outlived two husbands and become Baroness Bernstein. The twin brothers, George and Harry, find themselves on opposite sides in the American War of Independence. Historical figures such as General Wolfe and George Washington play some part in the novel but, despite the period research, it is the entirely fictional Beatrix who dominates it. *Barchester Towers* is a greater novel because of its artistic structure and human concerns. In his monograph on Thackeray Trollope wrote that the 'object of a novel should be to instruct while it amuses' and he added that it was a matter for decision whether 'this may be best done by the transcendental or by the commonplace'. Even allowing for the fact that there are limitations to these criteria, *The Virginians* is a good example of how a novel can fail.

In his excellent introduction to *Barchester Towers* Robin Gilmour observes (he is writing of Slope) that 'he cannot stand comparison with George Eliot's Amos Barton and Edgar Tryan in the contemporaneous *Scenes of Clerical Life*' (p. xxvi). This comparison is somewhat unfair. Slope is portrayed as a Cambridge-educated sophisticate who has also preached in London whereas Amos is a provincial, and Edgar Tryan has had London experiences which, told in retrospect, are singularly unconvincing. The time action of *Janet's Repentance* is early 1830s, that of *The Sad Fortunes of the Reverend Amos Barton* 1837–8, well before the period of *Barchester Towers.* Nor is there any comparison between cosy southern Barchester and midland Chilvers Coton and Nuneaton.

The characterization of Amos Barton has some subtlety. He is represented as a commonplace man blind to his wife's suffering and stupid and insensitive enough to make it worse by inviting the Countess Czerlaski to stay with them. Milly Barton works bravely through their poverty and eventually dies. The deathbed scene in which the children are led in to take leave of their mother is moving, though somewhat overdone. The character of Amos himself succeeds mainly because of his faults, and the scene also displays some fine rustic humour, a genuine sense of the gossip and atmosphere of the times, a poignant focus on Milly's nobility of character and a fine study in egoism in the person of the Countess. The latter finally, and fittingly, has her condescension broken by the outspokenness of a servant, and takes her leave. It is too late, for Milly is already dying. This relatively simple story has its moments, but George Eliot is, I think, imbued with a seriousness of intention which militates against realism. The author's voice is well in evidence, and the author's vocabulary is sometimes intellectually self-conscious. It is a long story reflecting a fine intelligence and imagination, humour, a narrative curve, all a promise of what is to come rather than an achievement.

Janet's Repentance is in a different category. It is profoundly realistic in terms of the presentation of the alcoholic, but redeemable, Janet and her brutal husband, the lawyer Dempster. Both are portrayed in psychological terms. Dempster is devoted to his mother (who takes precedence over Janet) until her death, and the childless Janet devoted to her husband until his violent beatings drive her to drink. There is a kind of chorus of friends, the minor characters being particularly well drawn. The battle against the evangelical intruder Edgar Tryan, who wants to hold a Sunday evening lecture (would Mrs Proudie have approved?), is orchestrated by Dempster with his wife's support. Janet, in fact, helps with the placards which cruelly ridicule the preacher and his intentions.

All this is secondary to Dempster's continuing deterioration and the further brutalizing of his wife.

Things come to a crisis when Dempster turns Janet out into the cold in her nightdress. She is cared for by a friend, Mrs Pettifer, who is a supporter of Tryan's. The latter is a positive influence on Janet, who promises to try to cure herself of her drinking. Meanwhile Dempster is thrown out of his carriage in a drunken state, and Janet returns to nurse him in his *delirium tremens*. He dies and Janet, tempted back into her old ways, resists. She forms a close relationship with Edgar Tryan. He, too, dies after exhausting himself in his work, and Janet lives on, a tribute to his example, to do good works for others.

This is the outline of the plot, but the treatment is searching, way ahead of its time in terms of the psychological penetration and analysis of human motives. The wisdom which informs George Eliot's later works is present here, and already there is a mature use of image and symbol, a moral tone which is tolerant and compassionate, a qualified optimism in the individual capacity for change. But, as so often in George Eliot, the idealist who characterizes the later fiction, such as Felix Holt or Daniel Deronda, is the least convincing character. Edgar Tryan's past is sentimentally, even melodramatically, invoked and his utterances are too good, too noble, to be true. Slope has none of his Christianity, none of his humanity, none of his dedication, but Slope breathes fallen humanity where Tryan fails to breathe life at all.

Janet's Repentance is an impressive early work by a writer Trollope greatly admired. His own work, as some critics have stressed, tends to become increasingly sombre with the passing of the years, but *Barchester Towers* has a lightness of touch, a satirical and ironic verve which George Eliot rarely reached, and when she did so, did so in passing. To be fair, Trollope himself did not sustain this essentially comic approach to fiction. What is remarkable is that in this sequence, which had been so man-handled by his publishers in terms of comment and alteration, he produced one of the great novels of his time.

Dickens was to maintain his pre-eminent position at least up to *Our Mutual Friend* (1864–5), his last completed novel. Among its predecessors were *Great Expectations* (1861), arguably among his finest works. George Eliot was to reach best-seller status and literary eminence with her next two novels, *Adam Bede* (1859) and *The Mill on the Floss* (1860), though her greatest work, *Middlemarch*, was not published until 1871–2. I have already referred to Mrs Gaskell, but a look back at *North and South* (1854–5) shows that her concerns and Trollope's are some distance from each other. It is not just the location of Manchester (Milton Northern), it is also Mrs Gaskell's determined Christianity which separates them. Trollope gives the impression of being broadly tolerant in an urbane way; Mrs Gaskell is tolerant, but she is socially serious, hardly surprising in view of the period of which she is writing. Mrs Gaskell's strengths are her ability to show character in development (here she is not far from Trollope), but her scenes are different in texture from his. Trollope's interiors have passion – take, for instance, Mrs Proudie or Eleanor face to face with the archdeacon. Mrs Gaskell's exteriors and interiors are replete with social division and suffering, such as the mob confrontation with Mr Thornton in which Margaret is injured, or the dead Boucher brought home on a door after drowning himself in a few inches of water. At this stage, this kind of realism is outside Trollope's range.

For Trollope *Barchester Towers* points the way into the 1860s and to his period of greatest popularity. As Hardy later was to create Wessex, so Trollope created a county with a nucleus of families and situations which would draw people's interests. The man he most admired, Thackeray, was never to recapture the imaginative power which was present in *Esmond*, *The Newcomes* and, above all, *Vanity Fair*. With his death in 1863 Trollope was gradually to take over Thackeray's position. It led to his being styled 'a lesser Thackeray', an unfair evaluation and taking no account of Trollope's variety. His is a high achievement, even at this stage. Michael Sadleir wrote in 1927 that 'the fine-combing of English country life revealed to Trollope the immense strategic strength of the social position of the upper clergy' (*Trollope: a Commentary*, p. 52). It is on this recognition that *Barchester Towers* is built, and when we add to it what Kathleen Tillotson has called Trollope's 'fertility of invention and skill in manipulating the intricate lines of his narrative' (*Introduction to Barchester Towers*, p. viii), we register that firmness of conception and artistic execution which marks the great novelist.

Conclusion

In the course of this examination of *Barchester Towers* I have referred several times to Trollope's *An Autobiography*, which reveals what Trollope thought about the art of fiction and about some of his fellow craftsmen. He had a clear conception of his own art and what he wanted to do.

A novel should give a picture of common life enlivened by humour and sweetened by pathos. To make that picture worthy of attention, the canvas should be crowded with real portraits, not of individuals known to the world or to the author, but of created personages impregnated with traits of character which are known. (I, p. 169).

or

I have regarded my art from so different a point of view that I have ever thought of myself as a preacher of sermons, and my pulpit as one which I could make both salutary and agreeable to my audience. I do believe that no girl has risen from the reading of my pages less modest than she was before and that some may have learned from them that modesty is a charm well worth preserving. I think that no youth has been taught that in falseness and flashness is to be found the road to manliness; but some may perhaps have learned from me that it is to be found in truth and a high but gentle spirit. Such are the lessons I have striven to teach; and I have thought it might best be done by representing to my readers characters like themselves – or to which they might liken themselves. (I, pp. 195–6).

We note the emphasis on character and morality, those twin pillars of Victorian fiction. It is true, I think, that the Barchester series is 'enlivened by humour and sweetened by pathos'. It is true, too, that Trollope is best remembered for his characters. Mrs Proudie, the archdeacon, Mr Harding and Madeline Neroni do not slip easily from the mind once encountered.

James Kincaid has accurately noted that *Barchester Towers* 'still contains a residue of the satire found in *The Warden*', while he also notes the 'vigorous and often subtle defence of the meek and the merciful' (*Introduction to Barchester Towers*, pp. viii–ix). Looking at him alongside his contemporaries Sir Walter Raleigh observed, 'Trollope starts off with ordinary people that bore you in life and in books, and makes an epic of them because he understands affection which the others take for granted or are superior about', quoted in Hugh Walpole's *Anthony Trollope* (1928). I suggest we consider 'he understands affection', for it seems to me that *Barchester Towers* reveals just that. He holds his characters in affection, he holds life in affection, he holds his readers in affection, and I believe he holds the art of writing in affection too. It is a modest quality, but when it is allied to a dedication to artistic creation, treated self-effacingly in *An Autobiography*, perhaps we should regard it as an important ingredient in Trollope's achievement, and certainly a constant feature in his practice.

Almost all books of criticism on Trollope suggest that there is a problem in his astonishing fecundity, his mechanical daily output of writing, the evenness of his style and the unevenness of his work, his lack of attention to plot and structure, image and symbol, his neutrality, the too frequent use of his own voice. The real problem lies, I suggest, with those critics who do not find it easy to place him because, like Dickens, he is inimitable. It is one of the measures of great writing that it survives its own time and delights, intrigues, stimulates, speaks positively to, subsequent generations. This commentary on *Barchester Towers* has tried to demonstrate the excellence of that novel, on the grounds of its artistic achievement and its humanity. I defer here to the words of R. C. Terry. His memorable book, called *Trollope: The Artist in Hiding* (Macmillan, 1977), aptly shows that Trollope is not 'the chronicler of small beer' which some would still have us believe. He defines 'what is great about Trollope in thought and execution':

> ... the scene richly patterned in incident, the texture of physical expression, movement and gesture, the subtleties of reflection, and the haunting reintroduction of motifs in the narration, of which only a glimpse can be had by short quotation ... perfect modulation of narrative voice and accurate dialogue ... a master-builder in prose ... He has left us cathedrals and palaces of fiction. (p. 248).

Further Reading

The books listed below have been found helpful.

Anthony Trollope, *An Autobiography* (Oxford, World Classics, 1983). Essential reading for anyone interested in Trollope, and particularly valuable for his account of his childhood, his attitude to and practice of the writing of fiction, and his views of his contemporaries.

Biography

Michael Sadleir, *Trollope: A Commentary* (1927), an important book in our understanding of Trollope.

James Pope-Hennessy, *Anthony Trollope* (1971), is the best of the biographical studies: lucid, informed, well researched. It has been issued in Penguin Books (1986).

Letters

The Bradford Booth edition of *The Letters* (OUP, 1951) has been superseded by N. John Hall's edition in two volumes: *The Letters of Anthony Trollope* (Stanford University Press, 1983). This is particularly interesting for students of *Barchester Towers*, since it contains the reader's report on the novel and detailed information on Trollope, his correspondents, and his times.

Criticism

I have found the following very useful:

Donald Smalley (ed.), *Trollope: The Critical Heritage* (Routledge and Kegan Paul, 1969, paperback, 1985).

David Skilton, *Anthony Trollope and his Contemporaries* (Longman, 1972). This contains some valuable analyses of contemporary criticism of Trollope, a more than useful supplement to *The Critical Heritage.*

P. D. Edwards, *Anthony Trollope: His Art and Scope* (Harvester Press, 1978). See, particularly, the focus on *Barchester Towers,* pp. 16–28.

James R. Kincaid, *The Novels of Anthony Trollope* (Clarendon Press, 1977). Stimulating discussion of the Barchester Chronicles pp. 92–142).

Bill Overton, *The Unofficial Trollope* (Harvester Press, 1982). Stimulating in many ways – biographically, historically, textually, and even has new manuscript material.

U. C. Knoepflmacher, *Laughter and Despair: Readings in Ten Novels of The Victorian Period* (University of California Press, 1971). A brilliant introduction and chapter on *Barchester Towers.*

Geoffrey Harvey, *The Art of Anthony Trollope* (Weidenfeld and Nicolson, 1980). Particularly good on the dramatic scene in Trollope.

R. C. Terry, *Anthony Trollope: The Artist in Hiding* (Macmillan, 1977). A finely perceptive and profoundly sympathetic study.

Arthur Pollard, *Anthony Trollope* (Routledge and Kegan Paul, 1978). A very good general introduction to Trollope's life and works.

John W. Clark: *The Language and Style of Anthony Trollope* (Deutsch, 1975). An interesting, exhaustive, scholarly and entertaining book.

Geoffrey Tillotson, 'Trollope's Style' in *Mid-Victorian Studies* (edited by Geoffrey and Kathleen Tillotson, University of London, The Athlone Press, 1965, pp. 56–61). Very good on the letters and admirably clear on its main theme: 'it is the style of one who knows how best to sustain grace without its seeming too much a thing of art'.

Texts

Robin Gilmour (ed.), *Barchester Towers* (Penguin). Excellent introduction and notes.

David Skilton (ed.), *Barchester Towers* (Pan Classics, Pan Books). Excellent introduction and notes.

James Kincaid (ed.), *Barchester Towers* (Oxford, World's Classics). Excellent introduction, notes by R. W. Chapman are sparse.

Kathleen Tillotson (ed.), *Barchester Towers* (Dent Everyman). Excellent introduction, no notes.

PENGUIN MASTERSTUDIES

This comprehensive list, designed to help advanced level and first-year undergraduate studies, includes:

SUBJECTS
Applied Mathematics
Biology
Drama: Text into Performance
Geography
Pure Mathematics

LITERATURE
Dr Faustus
Eugénie Grandet
The Great Gatsby
The Mill on the Floss
A Passage to India
Persuasion
Portrait of a Lady
Tender Is the Night
Vanity Fair
The Waste Land

CHAUCER
The Knight's Tale
The Miller's Tale
The Nun's Priest's Tale
The Pardoner's Tale
The Prologue to The Canterbury Tales
A Chaucer Handbook

SHAKESPEARE
Hamlet
King Lear
Measure for Measure
Othello
The Tempest
A Shakespeare Handbook

'Standing somewhere between the literal, word-by-word explication of more usual notes and the abstractions of an academic monograph, the Masterstudies series is an admirable introduction to mainstream literary criticism for A Level students, in particular for those contemplating reading English at university. More than that, it is also a model of what student notes can achieve' – *The Times Literary Supplement*